Add year: 20

The dent **s by turning people**

How to use your intuition for success in business. See Chapter 12

Do you suffer from sleep stupidity? Page 139

You can actively tap into your intuition. Find out how on page 126

The amazing coincidence that saved FedEx. Page 118

Do you need to bleach your mind? See page 100

Understand this basic principle and you are way ahead of the crowd. See page 96

The secret of the businessman who earned more profit from the goods he did not sell than from the goods he did sell. Page 82

How to become an instant expert in practically anything. Page 62

The difference between intelligence and IQ. Page 54

How to find your life's path. Page 47

The one thing you must do in using your intuition. Page 39

The one time you must never watch TV. Page 24

What every driver should know about falling asleep at the wheel. Page 128

Why you should be grateful for challenges. Page 189

Why were these women dropped from the space program? Page 165

How a good turn resulted in a life saving payback for the next generation. Page 152

The man who could not give his hand to save his life. Page 104

The one exercise you must not do under any circumstances. Page 102

A boy being expelled from school turns the situation to his advantage. What would you have done? Page 89

You can turn dead commuting time into higher income. Page 60

How a janitor became world famous by accident. Page 57

What babies fear most. Page 34

What influence did the ancient Roman Empire have on 19th century America? Page 17

Heed your inner warning system. Page 14

How to sleep better at night. Page 12

INTUITION

Your Secret Power

Your treasure map to the fortune that lies hidden in your mind.

Quentin Reynolds

DEDICATION

To every man, woman and child who against the dictates of conventional wisdom followed their true inner voice and blossomed towards their potential.

1 3 5 7 9 11 12 10 8 6 4 2

ISBN 0 9537144 0 3

Printed by Colour Books Ltd.,
Text Layout by Artwerk
Cover Design by Dunn + Associates
Cover photos by Mark Reddy of Norton Associates
Drawings by Terry Willers
Published by Adventures In Astonishment

Adventures In Astonishment
134 Custom Hall
Deverell Place
Dublin 1. Ireland.

Contents

WARNING

This book is designed to provide information to the subject matter covered. It is sold with the understanding that the publisher and author are not engaged in rendering legal, accounting, medical or other professional services. If expert assistance is required the services of a competent astrologer or psychic should be sought!!!

I said that to get you to pay attention. Seriously though, the content matter is designed to help you and point you in the right direction. But you must take responsibility for your own choices for it is only through so doing that you will achieve the freedom and growth that is your birthright.

INTRODUCTION

Read This First

Life was simple in the good old days. Only a few hundred years ago, you grew up in an area, rarely travelling more than twenty-five miles from your town, village or city. You probably stayed in the family business, generally agriculture. Most likely you were uneducated. Life was simple – certainly not easy – but simple. And, of course, the average life span was thirty years.

Today the average life span is heading towards eighty years; people are travelling all over the place. You can be on the other side of the world in less than a day. Communication technology means you can contact anyone, anywhere on the planet, instantly. People change careers at the drop of a hat. The average family changes home every five years. More people are going on to higher levels of education. The output of information is so large that even experts in their own field have difficulty keeping up with the latest developments.

So here we are, entering a new millennium, where technology is advancing so fast that whatever you buy today is out of date by next week. So while many aspects of life are physically easier, life itself is more complicated and certainly no longer simple.

That Overloaded Feeling

Do you feel work is piling up, your relationships are under strain, demands on your time are mounting, things aren't working out the way they should? Do you feel like getting away somewhere for a few days – on your own – locking the door, no phones, no newspapers, no television, no interruptions, no intrusions, just calm, peace and quiet? I'll bet you can feel the stress lifting just by thinking about it.

This book will show you ways to get in touch with your true self, which will lead to peace of mind, inner security and confidence.

You will discover how to eliminate the fears, worries and anxieties that crop up, how to bring flow, happiness and love into your life, how to use your natural creativity (of which you may be unaware) and how to tap into your intuitive power so that you will always come up with the right answer.

It is my contention that there is a flow to the universe. When you are in tune with this flow, everything in your life fits in place. It is like a well-tuned and well-lubricated powerful engine. For the engine to achieve peak performance all its parts must work well together. If one component is out of sync, the engine can still function but it is working against itself.

As you read through the book you will occasionally ask yourself, "What is this to do with intuition?" It is because I believe it is important to the whole process of using your intuitive intelligence and putting yourself in flow. Every little edge you can give yourself is important. Frequently the winning horse in a race is only a nose ahead of the runner up. Yet the winner receives by far the bigger purse.

Even just being a little more aware of your surroundings can give you that extra edge. This book is full of hints and tips to provide you with that advantage.

In Chapter 1, we look at the levels of awareness we humans have, leading to a discussion in Chapter 2 of what can help or hinder you in developing the intuitive process.

When you develop your purpose in life you are automatically on the right path. So many people are in jobs they hate, and are afraid or not sure how to find their true calling. You will discover how in Chapter 3.

You only need a little extra knowledge to be perceived as an expert and that can push you ahead of the crowd. It also increases your self-confidence and will help along your intuitive processes. Becoming an expert is simpler than you might think. Find out how in Chapter 4.

Learn in Chapters 5, 7 and 9 how to create a world that will put you into your flow, how to develop your intuition and understand your dreams.

Chapters 6 and 10 are full of techniques to turn apparent disaster, misfortune or setbacks into glorious opportunity, growth and triumph.

Sometimes, 'out of the blue' amazing things happen which make you think outside forces are at work. Learn to understand that coincidences are little bonuses. Ride with them. Read about them in Chapter 8.

Chapter 11. Beware of those with hidden agendas. Like termites in a wooden house, they will burrow inside your mind, making you feel you are in the wrong and will adversely affect your mental well-being. These people should be avoided at all cost.

Chapter 12 reveals methods of using your intuition for business success. This is the area in which most people are out of sync with their flow.

It is advisable, but not necessary, to read the book right through sequentially. You can dip in wherever you like. Feel free to disagree with anything I say. What is important is that you discover what is right for you.

I wish you every success.

Warmly,

Quentin Reynolds

CHAPTER 1

Your Four Levels of Awareness

Here's a proposition that has not occurred to most people. "All knowledge already exists." "Hang on, Quentin, how do you mean? Aren't you like the guy in the Patents Office in the nineteenth century who resigned because he felt everything had already been invented?"

Well, I don't think that everything has been invented. I doubt if everything ever will be. I am simply saying, "All knowledge already exists." It just has not yet been discovered. Each of the laws of physics always existed. They had just not been discovered. The same with the laws of technology. Every principle and law that will be uncovered by future generations already exists. They have not been found. Yet. If the process by which man can travel faster than the speed of light does exist, it is already there; we just have to develop it. It may mean discovering new laws of physics or a re-interpretation of existing laws. But my point is, if it is possible, the knowledge to do so already exists.

The great geniuses of mankind simply tapped into this knowledge. They were dealing with understanding, which up to that time was unknown to man. Newton revealed the laws of gravity, which already existed. Einstein developed his theory of relativity. Mozart, the musical genius, said he never wrote anything original in his life. He just wrote down what came into his mind, without any thought or effort on his part. In the play *Amadeus,* Salieri, while hostile to Mozart, is the one person who recognises that Mozart's work comes directly from the "mouth of God".

So there is a field of knowledge that is outside existing human perception, into which we can tap. It is from this that all discoveries have come, and all new knowledge and revelations will come. It is known by different names – infinite intelligence, the Christ consciousness, intuition, ESP, gut instinct, the inner voice, God, the spirit.

Whatever you choose to call it, however you regard it, you are aware of its existence. Even those who deny it cannot explain it away. Some fear it, some ignore it, and some point out you cannot prove it is there, but those who have tapped into it and used it are amongst the greatest people who have ever lived and their legacies are our gift. We can repay that gift by doing likewise.

You do not have to be a genius – at least not as you might perceive a genius to be. Later you will learn how you can operate at genius level, in your own way.

Everyone can identify with the hunches, the creative insights, the breakthroughs, and the apparently amazing coincidences that regularly occur to help us through life. We may be consciously unaware of them at the time; their significance only becoming apparent later. We can harness these intuitive processes for our benefit and that of mankind.

Tuition is knowledge; it is something you have learned that comes out of you. Intuition is knowing without logical thought; it is something you have not learned that comes to you. It is something you have free and clear. It is yours to use. Using it occasionally will give you an edge in your career and personal life that will put you in the top twenty per cent of society. Developing it further will catapult you into the top five per cent, up with the people who live on top of the pyramid where the air is clearer and the view is better, where there is less competition and more fun.

Finding the Key

Imagine discovering that the secret of life and the universe was hidden – locked away in a large safe, the key well concealed. You spend your whole life looking, searching for this key, following up every possible clue, combing the world, giving up everything until eventually you do find it. You return to the safe, insert the key in the lock and turn it. The rusty door creaks open. Inside is the secret of the universe. And what do you find when you look in the safe? What is this great secret? You find you, yourself. You had the secret all the time. It was there within you. You went elsewhere to find the key. The only place you did not look was inside yourself. That is the point of this book – to help you discover yourself, find yourself and to be you.

There is another story, the story of the Greek Gods. Legend has it that man was at one time equal with the gods. However, they became fed up with the abuse of his godlike powers, and decided to hide them. Discussing amongst themselves as to where they might conceal these abilities, one said, "Let's hide these powers at the top of the highest mountain. Man will never find them there." Another said, "No, no, sooner or later man will go climbing mountains and he will discover them. Let's hide them instead at the bottom of the deepest ocean." Interjected another, "He will find ways of exploring under the sea and will uncover these secrets. Let us stash them instead at the back of the deepest darkest cave." The wisest god counselled, "He will go looking and we know he will find them. Let us conceal them deep down in man himself, because that is the last place he will ever look."

Consider also the story of the "Acres of Diamonds". It seems that a farmer, who lived in Persia, was simply fed up running the farm. Hearing stories of great wealth he decided to be a diamond miner. He wanted to go and find his fortune – find and mine diamonds. Selling his farm he went off searching the continent for diamonds. He never found any, and eventually, in a fit of despair, threw himself into a river and drowned. In the meantime, back at the farm, the man who bought it was busy farming away. Crossing a stream one day he saw down in it a shiny object, which he took home and put on his mantelpiece. A few months later a holy man was visiting, saw the shiny piece of rock and began to examine it. The farmer explained that it had caught his eye glistening in the stream. "Well," said his visitor, "I think this is a diamond." They went and got it checked, and indeed it was. It was one of the biggest diamonds which had been discovered up to that time. Investigating further they found that the farm, which the first farmer had sold so that he could go looking for diamonds, was itself a huge diamond mine. One of the biggest and richest in the world – a mine that later provided the diamonds for the Crown Jewels of England and India.

The story of acres of diamonds is a very moving one because its moral is that what we are looking for is already under our feet. Once again, that is the point of this whole book. What you are looking for you already have. It is there; it is all around you. It is just a matter of tapping into it. You are going to discover many ways of doing just that.

If We Already Have All We Need, Why Do We Have So Much Difficulty in Finding It?

We can be so busy looking that we don't see the wood for the trees. For a moment, consider the tree. You see a tree standing alone in a field. You are aware of that which is the tree. Right? Well of course. You see the bark, the branches, the leaves, the entire tree. You see the space it takes up. Yes, it is a tree. There is no doubt about it.

But the tree is not solid. Most of what you perceive as the tree, between the branches, is empty space, just air. Compressing it in its entirety the volume would only take up a fraction of the space. So most of what you perceive as a tree, is in fact not a tree at all.

Let's take this further. The tree is also a home for thousands of insects; it hosts nests for whole families of birds. Squirrels may be in residence. Its blossoms provide nectar for the enterprising bee and other visiting insects. In the autumn, the tree yields its produce, be it fruit or nuts, which in turn is the seed for future generations of trees as well as providing food and nourishment for animal species. The leaves fall from the tree, decay and eventually become part of the soil which will later produce new life. Felling a tree can provide fuel, building material, floors, furniture, as well as the paper for this book.

Underneath is the network of roots, not to mention the worms, underground insects and burrowing animals. The network of roots is a mirror image of what you see above ground. Around it are the smaller plants, which rely on the tree for their own survival. Its trunk provides a means for cows and horses to scratch themselves, its outstretched limbs giving shelter to picnicking families and courting couples.

Next time you see a tree, contemplate on that which is the tree as well as that which is not the tree. You will begin to understand that when you look at yourself or another human being, there is so much more than would first appear.

What Roles Do You Play?

What are the roles you play in your life? You are a daughter or a son, a mother or a father, aunt or uncle, grandmother or grandfather. You could be a brother or a sister, a friend, cousin, distant cousin, brother-in-law, sister-in-law. You could be a teacher, a mentor or a student. Perhaps a manager, supervisor, employee, entrepreneur, mechanic, farmer, musician, technician.

You have multiple roles in life, each requiring a different perspective. Depending on which role you are playing, your actions and reactions will change, depending on who you are dealing with. You are so used to them, you probably don't even notice. For example you will speak differently to a child than an adult. You will speak differently to your spouse than your boss.

You also act in different ways depending on the mood you are in, your agenda and the time available. There are areas of your life you desire to keep covered and hidden, as well as areas that you have not yet discovered. One thing is sure; your potential is far greater than you think. The history of mankind is littered with people who have sold themselves short.

This book will help you become more aware of who you are, how to become more in tune with yourself, how to tap into your intuitive side, resulting in increased fun and prosperity in all areas of your life.

There is little point in solely covering intuition, while ignoring the other areas of consciousness. Each area works well on its own, but when used in collaboration with each other, they yield results that are infinitely more powerful than you can imagine. Learning to do this will put you operating on genius level. It will deepen your understanding of yourself and those around you. It will give you an inner power that can withstand outside hostile forces. You will inwardly know the right thing to do. This inner knowing will bring incredible peace of mind and the ability to look on problems as opportunities. It does not mean the rest of your life is plain sailing but you will have the inner confidence of knowing you can deal with it. As you make the first steps and see your progress, your trust and faith in yourself will grow exponentially, giving you that inner glow of "knowing".

We can divide our areas of awareness into four fields:

- Basic survival (animal) instincts dealing with our survival and procreation.
- The conscious mind dealing with rational logical thought.
- The subconscious being, the inner you.
- The superconscious, which is infinite intelligence, knowing without logical thought or reasoning.

A slightly different but easier way of looking at this is to see us on these four levels:

- Physical
- Emotional
- Mental
- Spiritual

The Physical

This covers our survival as both individual physical beings and as a species. We have inbuilt instincts for survival and procreation. Imagine yourself as an early man. You hunt in small groups, moving around looking for food. Predators or enemies from rival camps can set upon you. You have to be very much aware of your environment and what is going on around you. Your very survival depends on it. Verbal skills are minimal, so body language and symbols are the main means of communication.

Have you ever been somewhere, perhaps at a party and you became aware that someone, outside your field of vision, was staring at you? You couldn't know logically, but you sense it. You will frequently become aware of things that are going on around you, but you are not sure what they are, or why you perceive them. This is part of your animal instincts, part of your survival mechanism. These senses of survival are very highly developed in the wild animal kingdom. Ancient man could not have survived without them.

Part of the Chinese practice of Feng Shui (pronounced fung shway) is to do with the harmonious placement of furniture in your home. The theory is that "chi" which is the flow of energy, must be able to move freely around your abode. Especially interesting is the placement of your personal furniture. The chair you sit on, like your bed, should be facing the door and with its back to the wall. This is so that nobody can sneak up behind you, and no one can enter without you seeing him or her. If you must sit where you cannot see the door, then you should place a mirror on a wall reflecting the doorway, thus it can be seen from where you are sitting.

Centuries ago, we humans were more warlike. We were more physically active and we were hunters. An enemy might sneak up behind you, so it was necessary to protect yourself, and we still have these inner survival instincts. This is why in a room you feel safer and more secure when you can see the doorway. Likewise, your bed should be placed so that you can see the door, should anyone enter. And this may be why a lot of people do not sleep well at night. Their inner being is aware that they are not fully protected from possible danger. If you have sleeping problems, try re-arranging your bedroom furniture. Your inner being is there to keep you from danger, to protect you. Your inner bodyguard is there to keep you alert. If your inner bodyguard is not happy, you yourself cannot be at ease. Unhappiness or discontent in your inner being will manifest itself in irritability, sleeplessness or ill health.

Do You Have These Stress Symptoms?

A friend of mine ran a restaurant. It was busy and well run. It had good food at reasonable prices, very friendly staff, but it was not making enough money. He had to balance all the day-to-day running of the restaurant with seeing salesmen, accountants and bank managers while still working long shifts on the restaurant floor. Frequently the waitresses, from their tips, went home with more money than he did!

I called over one Saturday evening around closing time. He was in the office, doing the accounts for the day. "How's things?" I asked. "Well," he said, "I have a pain in my chest and have a kind of stiffness in my left arm. It has been building up over the last few days. I am going down to the hospital to have it checked out." Worrying, wouldn't you think? He was thirty-four at this time. I dropped him off at the hospital. We spoke the next day. "It wasn't too busy when I arrived around eleven-thirty," he said. "They took me in and did loads of tests. Eventually the doctor said, 'There is nothing wrong with your heart, nothing at all. It is just stress.' As soon as he said this I felt as if a huge weight was taken from me. All the discomfort went in an instant."

A few months later he was taken back into hospital for tests for another complaint. He was coughing up blood. Under general anaesthetic, he had a hole made in his throat and numerous tubes inserted through it into his lungs and stomach. The doctors did all the tests they knew, searching to see what might be wrong. They found nothing. Again, it was stress, just stress. Shortly afterwards he gave up the restaurant business and went back to his first love, which was cinema and screenplay writing, and is now much happier.

Some years ago, I had a theatre booked for two weeks after Christmas. I was doing two shows a day, each lasting an hour and a half. I was the sole performer. Every single day when my backstage team came in, something different would be wrong. There was always a difficulty or a problem, and it was always something stupid that could have been avoided by the theatre's own staff. Towards the end of the run, I was going home shaking. My whole body was trembling like an advanced stage of Parkinson's disease. I went to the doctor, who said he could find nothing physically wrong with me. It was pure stress, built up from just two weeks of dealing with incompetent people.

The lesson here is to go with the grain. What do I mean by this? Well, tear up a sheet of newspaper. Tear it in one direction and it will tear straight down from top to bottom. Tear it in another direction and it will tear all over the place. One way you are going with the grain, the other way against it. In life there is a flow for each of us. We can go with the flow or against it. Going against the flow causes problems, anger, stress and inner turmoil. Going with the flow, while it will often bring hard work, will also usher peace of mind, contentment and fulfilment.

In the above examples, my friend was dealing with problems that were difficult to overcome on his own. He was in a business, which while he was good at it, was not in his flow. In the theatre in which I was performing, which is with my flow, I was dealing with people who were unpredictable, sloppy and inefficient. It was this that was causing my stress. Incidentally one of the greatest causes of stress is not something you did; rather it is omitting to do something you should have done. The things you did not do. In my theatre show example I should have confronted the theatre management. Rather I chose to tell myself, "I am only here for two weeks. Don't make a fuss."

Those Little Bells

Can you identify with the little internal warning bells that caution you against getting involved with a person or situation?

I have frequently turned away from people, situations or potential business arrangements that looked good on paper. Somewhere inside me, little warning bells rang.

Occasionally they clanged. I can say that most times I have heeded them, without knowing why. On the occasions I ignored them, I soon discovered, to me detriment, why they were ringing.

I have discussed this with a number of friends and they have all had similar experiences. One got involved with a girl who was totally neurotic and another was lucky to escape from a situation with his life. The guy who got involved with the girl had a few drinks taken, yet can still recall the internal warning signals he chose to ignore.

If you get nothing else from this book please heed this advice: Your inner warning system is there to protect you. Somehow it perceives situations that are not obvious to the conscious mind. If it signals that "something is not right," pay heed.

We share our inner instincts with other living creatures. The instincts of survival, shelter, food and procreation, are very strong within us. Without them, we humans would have become extinct years ago. But we have other areas of consciousness not shared by any other species.

The Emotional

Nearly all our decision-making is made on an emotional level. We will give logical reasons to others to explain our choices, but the real hidden reason will be emotional. You might buy an expensive new car because it has a special trim or leather seats or it feels good. But you will never admit that to your friends. You will tell them, "Well, of course it has the latest ABS, it has the latest airbags and it is very safe." See? Giving logical reasons but buying for emotional ones. Some of the greatest traps in our lives are on the emotional level. If you can control your emotions rather than have them controlling you, you are automatically on a higher, richer, level. It is not as difficult as you might think, just requiring some minor adjustments in your thinking and the resolve to stick with these changes.

On a rational level, people pride themselves on their individuality, their uniqueness and originality, but on the deeper emotional level they are afraid of doing anything unusual. They fear the ridicule of being different from the perceived norm. Most times, this norm is a cesspit of mediocrity and there is safety in numbers. Look at people walking down the street. So many wearing clothes with blatant designer labels all over them. I think it is extraordinary that individuals will pay over the odds to wear clothes with advertising emblazoned all over it. Try to buy a plain sweatshirt or jog pants. It is almost impossible. Take more formal clothes. If they are exclusive and well made enough to justify the higher price, there should be no need to stick a designer label on the outside. An executive from the musical television industry was asked if his company had any influence over its viewers: "We own them, we tell them what to wear and how to dress."

Fashion's Got The Power

A poem by Pat Ingoldsby

If your mother had said to you years ago
"You are not leaving this house
unless you wear your cap back to front"
you'd have said –
"Ah ma...that's mental cruelty...
that's not fair...you're weird."

People had their heads shaved
either because –
(1) they'd been collaborating
with the enemy
(2) they had ringworm

At present
couples are not walking around
inside the same pair of jeans.

Give it time.

"We Always Do It That Way"

Many people hate change in any shape or form. They are set in their ways and dislike new ideas. They do things by tradition because they have always been done that way.

Have you heard the story about the recently married man whose wife was preparing a leg of lamb for Sunday lunch? She cut off the end of the leg of lamb before putting the leg in the roasting tin. He asked, "Honey, why are you cutting off the end of the leg of lamb?" She said, "I am doing that because my mother always cut off the end of the leg of lamb." "Oh," he says, "I wonder why she did that?" Well, she was visiting for dinner and when she arrived the son-in-law asked, "Mum, tell me why do you always cut off the end of the leg of lamb?" "Well, I always cut it off because my mother always did it." "Oh," he said, "let's phone Grandma and ask why she does it." So they phoned Grandma and enquired, "Hi grandma, we are making lunch here and we are just wondering why did you always cut off the end of the leg of the lamb?" She replied, "Because my roasting tin was too small." So, grandmother cut off the end of the leg of lamb because she had a good, logical and necessary reason to do so. She had to eat and she had to cook lamb, and that was the only way she could do it. Without realising why, her daughter and granddaughter started doing the same thing. It became what we call a tradition.

The Ancient Roman Railway of the U.S.

The distance between the rails on a railway track in the United States is four feet eight and a half inches. Why is this gauge used?

Workers from England built the first US railroads and they used the gauge from the old country. And the reason the English built them like that is because the early rail lines in Europe were designed and built by the same people who built the tramways, which were around before the railways, and they used that gauge.

Why then did they use it?

The people who built the trams used the same tools and jigs that were used for wagon building, which had the same wheel spacing. Wagons used that odd wheel spacing, because that was the spacing of the old wheel ruts on the old long-distance roads and when they had tried to use any other spacing, the wagons were prone to break down because they were the wrong spacing for the ruts.

So where did these old roads come from? Who built them?

The first long-distance roads in Europe were built by the Roman Empire for their Legions, and these roads have been used ever since. And the Roman war chariots first made the ruts, which everyone else had to use because they might otherwise destroy their wagons. The war chariots were all made to exact specifications for the Roman Empire and they were identical in wheel spacing.

And why did these war chariots have this specific wheelbase, four feet eight and a half inches?

Because the chariots were designed to be just wide enough to accommodate the rear ends of two warhorses.

So, the answer to the question is the United States standard rail gauge of four feet eight and a half inches comes from the original military specification for a Roman Empire army war chariot.

So are you doing things the same way today as you did them yesterday, for no good reason and perhaps still getting nowhere? Are you re-living past glories, real or imagined, because you are afraid to embrace today?

Your Self-Image

Our emotional reactions are largely governed by our self-image and our own personal rules. Self-image can be divided into two sections:

Comparison.

Self-esteem.

With **comparison self-image**, it means that I compare myself with you, my body with yours, my address with yours, my house with yours, my car with yours and I hurt inside because I don't have what you have. Comparison self-image means pain, hurt, loss, anger and feelings of being not good enough.

The **self-esteem** side is self-respect for yourself and it means freedom and love. You build your self-respect by making decisions that are right for you and your family, and not based on what other people think, or what you expect they might think.

Two channels, gaining pleasure or avoiding pain, control your emotional state. Most people will take steps to avoid pain rather than seizing the opportunity of gaining pleasure. Avoiding pain comes from fear. If you have an essay to do for school, the pain, discomfort and inconvenience means it gets put off until nearer the deadline, when the pain of not doing it becomes greater than the now relatively minor discomfort of doing it.

The emotions we choose to feel are based on our perceptions of reality, which in turn are based on our rules for the world. These in turn are often built on the rules and regulations imposed on us by others, our parents, school, religion and the government. Not conforming is risking the pain of rejection by your friends, family and society. Not wearing the fashionable clothes as worn by your peers invites jeering and ridicule.

Life itself is neutral and flows through you. Your emotional state depends on how you filter it. How you filter it depends on your own experience, your prejudices and your rules. Your feelings, whether you react or respond, are based entirely upon these rules. We can react negatively, bringing fear, anxiety, pain and stress, or respond positively, bringing love, care, help, healing and learning. Unfortunately, most of our rules lean towards feeling bad and few towards feeling good.

Add Years To Your Life Expectancy

So let's look at your rules and see how they can be put under your control. This will give you responsibility for your own emotions.

What are your rules for feeling happy?

Perhaps your boss has to praise you, someone has to give you a present or someone has to hug you. If so, other people are in charge of your rules and you are doomed to stress and hardly ever feeling happy. But if your rules for feeling happy are that you finish your current project, you smile at people, you eat your favourite food, then you are in charge of your rules. Feeling happy is under your own direct control, and away from outside interference. Look at all areas of your life and examine your rules for loving, feeling loved, feeling intelligent, being happy. The basic rule formula used by most people is:

For me to be ... (happy, loved), my boss, spouse, family must...
For me to be happy, my fellow workers must greet me by name every morning.

This is going nowhere. Change it to:

For me to be ... (happy, loved), I must...
For me to be happy, I must greet my fellow workers by their first names every morning.

Remember, every upset you have had with another person is an upset about your rules or their rules. You need to tell others your rules and ask them for theirs. Maybe your rule for feeling loved is to be hugged and your partner's rule is to be kissed. Both of you will feel unloved because you are not getting back what you need. When you get upset with yourself, it is because you broke one of your own rules.

Now one thing you don't need is too many rules and you certainly must examine your rules to make sure you don't have conflicting ones. Also check your rules to see if they empower or disempower you. If you have too many rules that you must always do this, or this always has to happen, you will stress yourself out.

When I give a speech, I know that about five per cent of the audience will not like me for whatever reason. It is the same for every speaker and entertainer. I could drive myself demented attempting to win them over. It is unlikely I would succeed, and in doing so I would probably alienate the rest of the audience. If my rule for a successful speech is that I have to connect with and inspire every person in the audience, I am doomed. If instead my rule is to give the best I can at that time and in these circumstances, then I am in control and inwardly happy.

This idea of controlling your rules for your emotions will eliminate enormous levels of negative stress from your being and thus add years to your life expectancy.

Learning to channel your emotions releases powerful forces from within. Negative emotions like envy, jealousy and hate will devour you from the inside, like a malignant cancer. If you turn negative emotions around you can use them as a launching pad. Great life changes occur when people become disgusted or fed up with the way things are. "I will not put up with this any longer." They resolve to change. The resolve to achieve your dream, your goal, and your life's purpose will propel you through apparently insurmountable obstacles.

The Mental Level

(a) The Conscious Mind

This is our conscious, thinking, rational, reasoning area. When you are awake and paying attention to what you are doing, your conscious mind filters all sensory inputs. It is actively analysing and deciding whether you agree or disagree, like or dislike the sensory inputs you are receiving, be it watching TV, listening to the radio, reading the newspaper, talking with someone, eating food – whatever.

If you ever observed somebody watching a political broadcast or a political interview, and the person being interviewed is somebody from the same political persuasion as the viewer, you will notice that the viewer will agree with everything that the politician is saying. If they are from another party with an opposite point of view, you will find that the viewer will disagree and ridicule the politician. An impartial observer, watching the politician, may not care either one way or the other, but will pick out some points that they agree with, and some that they disagree with. The first two are on the emotional level; the impartial observer is on the rational or conscious level. But they are still making the conscious decision that they either agree or disagree with the input of information.

Our rational thought, comes through our conscious mind, making logical sequential decisions. Our conscious mind also includes that part of us which is analytical, to do with all kinds of analysis, to do with logical problems and things that follow in a logical sequential order. It is that part of us that works out that if you do (a) followed by (b) followed by (c) followed by (d), you will get (e) and so on.

Learning in school mainly takes place on the mental level through reasoning and repetition. Our conscious mind operates a filing system, where information gets stored in an orderly manner that can be recalled quickly.

If we are talking about the Battle of the Bulge, which took place during the Second World War, your mind will instantly access its filing cabinet for history, go into the folder marked "Second World War" and find the file for the Battle of the Bulge. If you know nothing about this battle, your mind will still open up the filing cabinet on history, the folder on the Second World War, open a subfile on the Battle of the Bulge and input into that the information you are about to learn. Afterwards, it will all be filed neatly away for instant recall.

To Think or Not To Think

Most people, confronted with a problem, will never sit down and think it through. They will talk with their friends, the person beside them on the bus and frequently accept hearsay evidence from the most unlikely and unqualified source as gospel truth.

Have you ever had someone discuss a problem with you, to which you may be able to offer a solution or a path to a solution? You take the time to talk it through with them and inwardly you feel, yes, this is the way for them to go and if they follow this advice they must at least make some progress, if not solve the problem completely. Now you think they would say, "Well, thank you, that will help me solve my problem," but often what they will say is something like, "Yes, but my sister has a friend at work who says his uncle knew a man who did that and got fired from his job. On the way home he was hit by a bus and is now in a home for the bewildered. So I'm really not sure if that is the right answer." And this is presented back to you as a reason why they won't accept your suggestions! Earl Nightingale said some people would resort to anything, even crime, rather than sit down and think. Here are two suggestions to help clear thinking:

1. Think aloud. Talk the matter through with yourself.
2. Use a pen and paper. Write down the problem or worry. Write down the worst thing that can happen and all the other possible outcomes that you can think of. Write down ways of overcoming the problem. You will find a lot more on this in chapter 5.

(b) The Subconscious Mind

You can, with little effort, put your thinking abilities to their best advantage. The conscious mind is only part of the process. The other major part of the equation being the subconscious.

The subconscious works hand in hand with the

conscious, but operates completely differently. While the conscious is logical and organised, the subconscious accepts everything that goes into it. That is a very important point. The subconscious cannot analyse or reject any input. It accepts everything. Therefore you have to be so careful what you let into it.

Of course, you cannot monitor everything, as the subconscious is always working day and night from the moment you are born. All the subliminal messages from your friends, family and environment are absorbed by it. If as a child you are constantly told by people you respect and trust, such as your parents, that you are stupid or clumsy or always doing the wrong thing, over time your subconscious will accept that as truth and you will act in the way you are conditioned. Seeing yourself as stupid or clumsy you will act the way that is expected of you.

While the information in our conscious mind can be accessed logically, what goes into the subconscious mind is like an untidy filing system. Everything is thrown in the corner, heap upon heap upon heap, and when you need an idea, you have to let it do the sifting. You cannot access the subconscious filing system in a logical manner.

The Time Not to Watch TV Is When You're Not Watching It

The most dangerous time to watch television or listen to the radio is when you are not paying any attention to them. When you actively watch TV or pay attention to the radio, your conscious mind is filtering the information. If you are not paying attention to the TV and radio, the subliminal messages are going straight in and influencing your subconscious mind. One or two inputs of this probably won't make much difference but over time such influences will build up and put messages you may not want straight into your subconscious. This is one of the reasons why hypnosis works. What happens is that the hypnotist relaxes your conscious mind. Your filters are turned off. The hypnotist is talking directly to your subconscious and putting in suggestions, which it accepts.

> ***"Clients visit me hoping that I will put them in a trance and fix their lives. In fact many of them live in a trance and need a dose of reality."* 'Tony Sadar, hypnotist'**

Your subconscious mind is always working. Let's say your name is Margaret. Imagine you are out in a restaurant with some friends, there is a conversation going at your table and you are actively involved in it, apparently paying no attention to anything that is going on elsewhere in the restaurant. At the table behind you there is another group having their own conversation. During it, if one of them happens to mention "Margaret" which is your name, your subconscious will alert you that perhaps they are talking about you. Your conscious mind will break off from your conversation and you will start to listen to the people behind you, just to see if it is indeed you they are talking about. If it isn't you will just ignore them, returning to the conversation at your table.

But isn't it fascinating that your subconscious would pick up on your name, uttered at another table? The next time you are in a busy restaurant or a crowded place, focus your attention on another table or group and listen to what they are saying. From where you are you may think you won't be able to hear anything, but by focusing and concentrating you will pick up what they are saying. Now, I say this, not that you should be eavesdropping, but just to train yourself to be more aware of what is going on around you.

The Steps to Competency

Generally speaking we learn new skills consciously and then put them into our subconscious mind where they get done without thinking. Learning can be divided into two sections, the competencies and the incompetencies.

A baby wearing shoes does not know that it cannot tie its shoelaces. It is an unconscious incompetent. It doesn't know that it doesn't know that it can't tie laces. As the child grows it becomes aware that it cannot tie its shoelaces. It does not have the skill. So it becomes a conscious incompetent – it knows that it doesn't know. You then get to the stage where the child starts to learn to tie its own shoelaces and it becomes what we call a conscious competent. It knows it knows how to tie its laces and it goes through the steps every day, concentrating on what it is doing. With practice it reaches the stage of becoming an unconscious competent. You just tie your shoelace without thinking about it and you can even do it while performing another task. It does not require your attention any more. It has been programmed and embedded into your subconscious mind.

It is the same when you are learning to drive. You quickly reach the status of a conscious competent. You know you are learning, and it is very jerky while you are going through the series of manoeuvres to drive off. But, as you acquire proficiency, you do this without thinking. Subconsciously you are driving the car and sooner or later you will reach the stage where you can drive from A to B and not even remember or recall the journey, because your subconscious mind has taken over.

Suddenly I Knew

The American psychic investigator James Randi started his career as a professional magician. In a conversation with the then top American magician Harry Blackstone, Randi bemoaned the fact that he hadn't achieved the competency he felt he should have. Blackstone replied that indeed Randi would eventually achieve it. Randi asked, "Well, how will I know?" Blackstone answered, "You will walk off the stage one day and you will know. You will just know." One night a few years later Randi was leaving the stage and he had that inner surge of excitement and he said to himself, "Hey, now I have it!"

When I learned Punch and Judy and put it into my show, I was quite happy with the way it was going. But it was six years later that I finished a performance one day and as I walked out from behind the puppet booth to see the audience, I felt that inner feeling, "Now I can do it!" What was different between that show and the show the day before? I really don't know, but there was an inner feeling that I knew I had truly mastered the craft.

Paul Daniels, the famous English magician whose top-rated TV series ran for sixteen years, had a similar experience. Early in his career, he was working on a trick with a cup and a ball. He had it in his show for three years and he just couldn't get the hang of it. He was changing a little bit here, changing a little bit there. One night, he walked offstage and he said: "That's it!" The routine has since become his signature piece, it's known as the "Chop Cup". He opens all his live performances with it and since that special night he hasn't changed one word or one little bit of the whole trick.

Knowing vs. Learning

Knowing how is not learning. I know how to play the violin. You rub the bow over the strings and music is created. But I could not play a tune for you if my life depended on it. I have not learnt the violin. In the early years of the twentieth century an amateur magician told David Devant, the top English magician of his day, that he knew thousands of tricks. Devant replied that he only knew ten. Of course Devant knew the secret to thousands of tricks; his point was that he had learnt ten. He knew them inside out and when Devant performed you saw "real" magic.

Most people today want instant gratification, they want instant this, instant that – they want to learn to do this now, they want to be able to do it by this evening. No skill worth having comes easily. Time, effort and practice are mandatory. The inner joy of rising above the mediocre and achieving something that is unique to you will give you more inner satisfaction than owning a hundred houses.

The Spiritual

This is the area where we tap into our superconscious mind. It gives us insights into infinite wisdom and infinite intelligence. This is the area of all knowledge. Some people feel that this is getting in touch with God, some people feel it is getting in touch with their inner being, the real person. Certainly when you tap into this area there is a feeling of awe and awareness.

Your subconscious deals with things you already know; things from your own personal experience. All the information, all the knowledge you have gained over the years, all your worries, the things that make you happy, all your emotions, have all been stored away in your subconscious. On the other hand, the superconscious taps into things that are outside your existing knowledge and experience.

Look at the ocean. Imagine that your creator took a glass and scooped some water from the ocean. You are the glass and what is in it. The glass is your physical body and the water in the glass is your spiritual side. Now, everything that is in the glass is exactly the same as everything that is in the ocean, because they are one and the same. The only thing separating them is the glass or our physical bodies. Tapping into your superconscious would be the same as tapping into the ocean.

You might also imagine that all minds are part of one Mega-Mind – or web. Imagine a spider web of infinite size whose strands connect everything that exists. You and I are tiny specks attached to the web. As the web is infinite, a vibration happening at point A does not simply travel to point B. It happens simultaneously all over. In the western world we are programmed to view ourselves as separate from the environment, humanity and the universe. Perhaps it is the web that is real and our illusion of separateness that is false.

History is overflowing with instances of individuals unexpectedly feeling connected to a higher learning, a deeper understanding, a revelation. In his book "*The Portrait of the Artist as a Young Man*," James Joyce describes this as an "epiphany". It is a moment of sudden and great revelation, when the hero understands what life is all about.

I experienced a minor epiphany aged twelve in maths class. For the last two years of junior school, maths, formerly one of my better subjects, was an ongoing horror. I could not grasp it at all. Algebra was difficult but algebraic division was unfathomable. I regularly had bad dreams about maths and dreaded that I would not pass the exam into the senior school. My new maths teacher was Fr Gerry Spillane. I remember vividly the first day he covered division in algebra. As he began his computations on the board I could suddenly see exactly where he was going. There was no doubt, no confusion and no difficulty. What had been dark and obscure suddenly became clear and obvious. The veil was lifted. It was, for me, an amazing experience. For the following six years Gerry Spillane was my maths teacher and he never had to explain anything more than once to me. We were tuned in to the same wavelength.

Helen Keller, the blind and deaf girl experienced an amazing revelation at the hands of Ann Sullivan, her teacher. Ann, herself raised in an asylum, is teaching Helen the letters for words. Helen cannot make the jump from letters to words and that the words mean certain objects. This is magnificently portrayed in the film "*The Miracle Worker*" starring Anne Bancroft as Ann Sullivan and Patty Duke as Helen.

Ann has Helen by the pump and is pouring water over her arms, at the same time spelling out the letters W A T E R on her hand, over and over again. It is a very emotional moment as Helen experiences an "epiphany" and realises that the letters mean the word, which means water. In that amazing moment a whole new world and a whole new life is opened to Helen.

"The only thing about a man that is a man is his mind. Everything else you can find in a pig or a horse."
Archibald McLeish, *playwright,*
The Secret of Freedom

CHAPTER TWO

Paradigms, Perceptions and Prejudices

Let's now have a look at intuition. Here are a few definitions for you to consider: intuition is the capacity to know without logical reasoning; intuition is the ability to make up your mind without knowing all the facts (prejudice is making up your mind without regard to any of the facts); intuition is a superior way of knowing ultimate truth without the use of prior knowledge or reason; intuition is a faculty of perception that is beyond the body, the emotions and the mind; intuition is knowing but not knowing how or why you know.

Your intuition can assess a situation far more accurately

than the logical conscious mind. Women are exceptionally good at this. At a social gathering, they will quickly realise the relationships between different individuals. While men would be more likely to analyse things and people, a woman will tend more to let the situation reveal itself to her. Exercises for developing these abilities are covered later in the book. This faculty for understanding will give you an immense advantage in creativity and decision-making. Learning to use and trust your intuitive self will take you to a different plane.

A note to men – you already have this ability, just your conditioning has trained you to assess situations differently.

The Watch Paradigm

A paradigm is a model or typical example of something. We all have paradigms for what we expect things to be. In the 1960's the Swiss had over eighty per cent of the world market in watches. Their paradigm was that watches had to be clockwork. They were fascinated by the delicate mechanisms and the centuries of tradition that went into their manufacture. Their own scientists developed the digital watch technology. However, it was outside their perceived paradigm. Believing it to be of little use, they gave it to the Japanese. People in the real world had more interest in the cheaper, more accurate watches that resulted. The marketplace shifted, the paradigm for watches changed and the Swiss had the rug pulled from under them. They now have about ten per cent of the world watch market.

What is your paradigm for running? Would you run five miles, ten miles? Would you run a marathon? Is that how far anyone would run? In our culture, running a marathon of twenty-six miles is a formidable achievement. Wow! Well done. Tell that to the Tarahumara Indians from the Mexican Sierra Madre Mountains. They regularly run up to seventy miles to attend religious festivals. For them seventy miles is the norm. A different paradigm.

What is your paradigm for the value of a book? Is it of value? Are you reading for entertainment or knowledge? An author may put a life's experience into a book. How much is that worth?

I believe that developing intuition is like learning any skill. Like all skills, some people are more naturally talented than others. But there is no skill that cannot be learned, assuming you are physically capable of it.

The Power of Shifting the Paradigm

Using your intuition requires no physical skills but some barriers are your current prejudices and paradigms. A few years ago, while appearing at the Dublin Horseshow, I came across a four-year-old boy crying. "What's wrong?" I asked.

"I'm lost."

"No you're not," I replied.

"I am, I'm lost."

"Who are you with?"

"My mother."

"Well, now you are with me, I know where we are, so it's your mother that's lost." The logic of this calmed him down. "Where did you last see your mother?" He showed me where. "We will wait here for a few minutes and if she doesn't show up, we will make an announcement and let her know where you are." The story ended happily with the distraught mother showing up a minute later. I had simply reframed the boy's paradigm. Like this small boy who believed he was lost, your perceptions of the world may need reframing.

When I did personal intuitive consultations, one pattern emerged from women clients in their forties and fifties. They had stayed at home to rear the children and now that the older ones had left and the younger ones were teenagers, these ladies wanted to develop some kind of career or, at least, part-time work. Their husbands were having major difficulties accepting this. Perhaps the husbands felt challenged as the breadwinner. Perhaps they felt the neighbours would think they were not earning enough and had to send the wife out to work to pay the bills. The men need to realise that everyone grows and changes. The wife wanted to grow to her potential. In nine cases out of ten, the husbands were refusing to even talk about it. The husbands were thinking from the comparison self-image. What others might think, rather than the mindset of "Let me help and encourage my wife grow into a more fulfilled human being." The husbands need a different paradigm.

Another woman had put a baby girl up for adoption. Later she got married and had three wonderful children. Yet, her focus was on the adopted child, thinking about her and what she might be doing, worrying if she were all right. These thoughts were burrowing deep into her subconscious. I counselled that by worrying about the child she didn't have contact with, she was subconsciously blocking out the three children she did have. When I pointed this out, it was as if a weight were lifted from her shoulders. She saw the reality of the situation. She knew, sooner or later, she would meet with her adopted daughter and could "let go" until that time came. By reframing her situation she could focus her love on what she did have.

Like with the Swiss watches, a shift in the accepted paradigm can completely change an industry. A shift in your paradigms can completely change your life.

What Babies Fear Most

Research has shown that babies have only two fears. Every other fear we have has been taught to us by others or we learn it from our own experience. Each of them can of course be unlearnt or at least dealt with face on. The two things babies fear? Falling and loud noises.

How Prejudiced Are You?

It has been said that prejudice is a wonderful thing. It enables you to make your mind up without knowing any of the facts. Watch out for the little prejudices that creep into your conversations. "Well of course he'd say that, he's a man, he's a Catholic, he's Jewish, he's black, well he supports that party, he's Irish."

Misinformed prejudices against yourself are serious obstacles to your success. Many of these are learned from your family, especially political, racial and religious prejudices. In the mid-seventies I did a number of shows at the Glencree Reconciliation Centre. A former British army camp in the Dublin mountains, it has been restored and is now used as a centre for peace and reconciliation. Initially groups of children from disadvantaged areas in Northern Ireland would get a week's holiday there over the summer months. Most of these boys and girls had close relatives killed or in prison. Children from Catholic and Protestant families were mixed together. At the start they would be extremely wary of each other, believing the lies, fears and hatreds they had been brought up with. Slowly they would mix, ending up the week sleeping in each other's arms. The week frequently ended in tears as they realised they were returning to ghetto life and continuing the new friendships was not a possibility.

Prejudices narrow your vision. They limit your focus on what you think exists or should exist, rather than what might exist or does exist. Your creativity will be stifled, narrowing your focus to one possibility rather than the endless possibilities. Prejudices build walls and barriers. They become a major obstacle to problem solving. Your mind will filter out new information and block its influence. You will see what you believe, rather than believe what you see. This leads to "in-the-box thinking". You limit your options and possibilities. All progress in the field of human endeavour came from people who thought "outside the box".

Everyone has a choice. Stay in the box and stagnate or step outside the box and evolve. The box, by the way, is an imaginary one, entirely of your own manufacture. There are limited, comfortable, prejudiced beliefs in the box. Outside, you will find challenges, unlimited potential and growth. You can of course always choose to do nothing, which is really the same as staying and stagnating. But it is your choice.

Assuming your goal, in reading this book, is to develop your intuition, we will concentrate on the right attitudes that will encourage your intuition to develop and the procedures that will allow it to do so.

In classical mythology, the hero encounters major obstacles in his search for the prize, which in all the better stories, he achieves. His greatest obstacles, though, are those within himself. These are the ones he really needs to overcome to win. The greatest obstacle to finding and using our intuitive ability is our lack of consistent belief in it. So we have to overcome this.

We Can Divide Intuition into Two Types:

Pure intuition. Intuition in its purest form is the threshold of spirituality. This is a perception of an essence, a principle or a truth on the spiritual plane, and is essentially inexpressible through words or descriptions. Pure intuition is in itself a spiritual experience.

Applied intuition. This is the application of intuition to the concerns of the personality, be it in relationships, professional work, science, art etc. Intuition can assess the information gathered by the senses, feelings and thoughts, and integrate them to arrive at a wiser and faster decision or conclusion.

Applications of Intuition

Assessing situations for decision-making. Intuition is an invaluable faculty for making major life decisions, such as:

- deciding to move abroad or to a new house;
- entering into a business partnership or deciding who you should marry;
- assessing the worth in investment of time in undertaking long-term projects;
- evaluating people such as job applicants or a judge in a court;
- accepting or rejecting opportunities in life such as promotion, trips, etc.

Alexis Carrel, Nobel prizewinner in medicine writes: *"All great men are endowed with intuition. They know, without analysis, without reasoning, what is important for them to know. A true leader of men does not need psychological tests, or reference cards, when choosing his subordinates. A good judge, without going into the details of legal arguments and even, according to Cardozo, starting from erroneous premises, is capable of rendering a just sentence. A great scientist instinctively takes the path leading to a discovery."* (Man the Unknown)

In interpersonal relationships. Intuition helps us to understand other people much deeper than their surface behaviour. We can feel or sense when another person is deeply troubled or whether or not the person is being honest and truthful.

Understanding deeper natural principles. Logic has its limitations. In understanding deeper principles, intuition is needed as a faculty that can synthesise. Discoveries in chemistry, physics and other fields have been attributed to intuition.

Albert Einstein: *"There are no logical paths to these laws, only intuition resting on sympathetic understanding of experience can reach them."*

John Maynard Keynes on Isaac Newton: *"It was his intuition which was pre-eminently extraordinary. So happy in his conjectures that he seemed to know more than he could possibly have any hope of proving. The proofs were dressed up afterwards; they were not the instrument of discovery."*

Understanding spiritual truths. Seeing deep truths in religious beliefs and spirituality requires insight that transcends logical thinking. You will meet many logical thinkers who can give you a thousand facts about religion but inwardly they know little or nothing about spirituality or love.

Imagine a series of concentric circles with you as the centre. These represent your sensory inputs. The first is taste, which takes place in your mouth, with your tongue. The next is touch, which takes place with your entire body. The next smell; further away again is the boundary of the hearing circle, then the outer circle for sight. That is the limit of our physical sensory inputs. Beyond that again is our intuition, which can only be accessed through our minds.

You may have heard the expression that we only use ten per cent of our minds. This is not to be confused with our brains. Take away some of those and you may well be dead or not able to fully function. There is little doubt that we are not using the full potential of our minds. At our stage of evolution there is a limit to where our minds can go. There is no limit though to what you can attract to you by using your subconscious and superconscious to their fullest advantage. We will cover this in depth in Chapter 7.

When I am talking about the logical mind I am referring to the conscious, reasoning, analytical part. The subconscious is the inner you, your dreams. It holds all the experiences you have ever had. The truly intuitive side is the superconscious, the infinite intelligence we can tap into. It is there where all knowledge already exists. For practical purposes, when I say use your intuitive side, or "let go", your mind will be tapping into either or both the subconscious and the superconscious. It does not matter from where the answer or inspiration comes, what matters is that you get it.

Do Not Neglect To Do This

There are two extra things you must do. You must act on the intuitive answer you get. If you do not follow through, your inner mind will not take you seriously. Suppose a friend contacts you. He has an urgent problem. A specialised training video is needed and he can't locate it anywhere. Can you help? With your connections you track one down. It takes you half a day. You could have been doing other things, but you want to help your friend. You bring the tape to his house. You call back a week later. The video is on the table, still sealed. He hasn't watched it. How would you feel? Used? Supposing he had a similar request every week for a few weeks. You still help out, but your friend doesn't act on what you do for him. Pretty soon you would be fed up with this and wouldn't bother. You would switch off, wouldn't you?

When you got the video, if your friend had said, "Thanks very much, I really appreciate your help, sit down. We are going to watch this straight away. There is a great idea on this tape." Supposing you get an idea from the tape that you can use to solve a problem in your life. Wouldn't you be thrilled? You might well be regularly contacting your friend asking if he needs more help. You would certainly be keeping a lookout for similar tapes containing equally good ideas.

Your subconscious responds the same way. Use the information it provides and next time it will be like a small child, eager to help. Once it sees you are serious, it will start to produce ideas regularly. Some will be good, some brilliant and some not very practical. If it gives you an idea for a pressing problem you must act on it straight away. Some ideas though, no matter how brilliant, you will not be able to use immediately. Write all these down in a journal or notebook. This is acknowledging the subconscious. You let it know you appreciate the ideas.

The other thing you must do is to thank your subconscious for its efforts. I know it sounds daft, thanking yourself. Your subconscious thrives on appreciation.

The basic guidelines for using your intuition are to use your logical conscious mind to work out what the exact goal is.

- One, write it down as concisely and specifically as possible.
- Two, assemble and study all the available data.
- Three, see if you can find a logical conclusion as sometimes the answer will be obvious.
- Four, if there is no immediate solution, let it go.

Points to Help Your Intuition

1. Only a small part of our mental activity takes place in ordinary consciousness.
2. Our perceptions are heavily influenced by our beliefs. In turn, our beliefs are influenced by suggestions we receive, especially those regularly repeated. Using affirmations such as "I am a great salesman," or "I like myself," on a daily basis will help change your self-image for the better.
3. We do not know what we really want, and we resist what we truly desire. Would you like to go to Heaven? Imagine you are standing outside a door marked "HEAVEN". Yes, this is it. Inside is everlasting happiness, complete peace, infinite intelligence and pure love. Picture the scene in your mind. You are at the door. You know heaven is on the other side. Now really visualise this door. You are going to open the door

and walk in. Pause a moment. Now do it. Open the door wide. Walk in. Would it surprise you to know that most people can't do it? Some can't even get as far as opening the door. Yet inside is pure love and happiness. Isn't this what we want?

4. We all have access to our intuitive and creative abilities, which are infinite. We are not all fighting for a share of a limited pie. You can breathe in all the air you can. It will not affect anyone else. There is more than enough. The oxygen in the air is constantly replenished by the plant life every day. Likewise you cannot use up the abundance of the universe.
5. The intuitive side is always available. All your decisions should be intuitive ones. Even obvious, logical decisions should be referred to the intuition to see if it feels right.
6. It is entirely reasonable that your higher self, with its access to infinite wisdom, may have a plan – a purpose for you, for your day, for your life.
7. The plan will be in harmony with the ultimate wellbeing of you, those around you and the universe.
8. All the resources needed to implement this plan will be made available to you. This does not mean they will land in your lap while you are sitting on your butt. It means when you are in action, doing, implementing your plan, doors will be opened to you.
9. Paying attention to and implementing this plan will lead you to a higher level. If followed with integrity, there will be an accompanying inner peace, a sense of oneness with all about you and an inner sense of joy.

Things to Watch Out For which may Hinder Your Intuition from Working

1. You value your comfort zone too highly. You feel it is easier to get by as you are, rather than make the effort for the better things in life.

2. A belief in separateness will hinder you.
3. You must have the willingness to let your intuition work.
4. You must listen to no other voice.
5. Is your intuition telling you something you don't want to know? Perhaps it is anticipating a relationship is about to end, and you don't want to face the facts.
6. Don't let your prejudices speak. Are you reacting too quickly without even assessing all the available facts?
7. Is your ego in the way? Do you want all the kudos? It is amazing what can be achieved when you are prepared to share or allow someone else to take the credit.
8. Worrying about what others think. This is a major obstacle to success in any field.
9. Don't underestimate yourself. You have more capabilities than you can imagine. After you have used your intuition a few times on simple things your confidence will grow.
10. Don't expect too much at the start. Build on small successes. A building is built one brick at a time, from the bottom up.
11. Are you afraid of what your intuition might reveal? If there are deep traumas from your past, you may need professional counselling to release those demons. Your superconscious, the spiritual side is there to help and guide you not to put obstacles in your way.
12. Are you misinterpreting your intuition? Are you seeing what you want to see, or expect to see, rather than what is being revealed?
13. Do not let outside influences force your decision. Family pressure can be very strong. Are you becoming a doctor because you want it, or your family does? Perhaps you are engaged and your marriage announced. Yet your inner voice is telling you not to go through with it. Do not make a lifelong mistake because of social pressure.

14. Intuition works best when used with your thinking mind. They complement each other, and the resultant whole is greater than the sum of the parts. Do not skip the logical exploration of the question.

By encouraging your mind to think beyond the obvious you are opening the door to an Aladdin's cave of new experiences, wealth and wonder. The extraordinary thing is that you already have this and it is simply a matter of tapping into it. Remember the important points in learning something new are your purpose, your attitude and the procedure. In the next chapter we'll start with your purpose. If you refuse to use your mind to bring you abundance, you deserve to be poor and stupid.

Ideas are like slippery fish; if you don't harpoon them – with your pencil – they get away. **Earl Nightingale**

CHAPTER 3

Finding Your Life's Path

> ***"Perhaps real individual failure lies in the squandering of potentiality, a volitional waste of one's ability. If you paint signs when you could paint sunsets, invent jingles when you might compose symphonies, foregoing eventual achievement in favour of instant reward, that may be regarded as personal failure."***
> **Bob Monkhouse**

The Terror of Choice

Things are always growing, developing, maturing. We, as people, are in a constant state of growth and change. And, of all the beings of this planet Earth, we have free will. We can make choices. We are also very much aware of a side of our makeup that is not physical. This is an area that allows us to be creative, solve problems, help others, invent and grow as individuals, to fulfil our destiny.

A tree will always be a tree. It does not opt to take a year out from growing. It does not determine, "Hey, this year I will be a flower or a bush." No, it continues to be a tree. Dogs do not choose to be cats, nor does a cow decide this year to be a horse. They are each true to their nature.

So the question is, are you true to your nature? Your life is yours to live. It is your play to write. Do you want the leading role in your play? Or, would you rather have a small, perhaps insignificant, part in somebody else's? If you choose to be in someone else's play, you have no control over the plot, the direction, the passage or the end result. If your choice is to take hold of your life, write your play and star in it, you will have riches, wealth, fulfilment, peace of mind and happiness that are not realised by ninety-five percent of the population. If you choose to be the author of your own destiny, you will find an awareness, an inner feeling of contentment that is not really describable. If the choice of personal fulfilment is yours, if your choice is a voyage where the ultimate destination is you, then this book will help you chart the way.

Did you see the play *Dancing at Lughnasa*? It is the tragic story of four sisters living in rural Ireland trapped in a prison entirely of their own making. Is your choice to be a victim? So many people choose to stay as victims in other people's lives. They relinquish the lead part in their own. How many stay in unworkable relationships? In this position it is easier to do nothing, for if you do nothing, you are not taking any responsibility. Some call it the comfort zone. But it is certainly not comfortable – far from it. It is the familiar zone, we are used to it. The devil you know is better than the devil you don't know.

Now, there is a better way. You really can go for everything you want, and the best part is that you already have everything you need. Yes, read that again! You already have everything you need. You have a mind, instincts and intuition.

The Vital Question

What do you want to do with your life? Some people are very lucky, they know straight away – hey, I really like music, I want to be a musician – and that is what they do for the rest of their lives. There is no doubt about it, they know from a very early age – I like music, and this is going to be my career – and they dedicate their life's work to that.

But even more people are not sure what they want to do. "Mmm – I don't know, I might like to do this, I might like to do that – I don't know," is what you hear them say. "I haven't found anything that I really like doing – I don't know, I think I might like to but I don't know whether I should spend four or five years studying it in university and then discover that I don't like it."

Here are the Eleven Steps to Discovering Your Life's Path

1. What do you like doing more than anything else? Turn this into your life's career. If your natural inclination is towards music, you should learn everything you can, study everything you can about music, learn the instrument that you like playing, study the theory, practice, if necessary get together with other like-minded people, form a band, form a group. If music is in your blood, you will not be happy unless you are playing music. A poet will not be happy unless he is writing

poems. A writer will not be happy unless he is writing books. Somebody who likes flying will not be happy unless he is flying. So whatever it is, whatever really is your passion in life, work out how to make your living doing that. There you will find fulfilment. Commit yourself to that and away you go!

2. What would you do if you won the lottery? If you suddenly became financially independent and you would have no money troubles for the rest of your life? You can live wherever you want, you can do whatever you want. What would you do with your time? What work would you involve yourself in? You might decide, oh well, I will go on a holiday – I have always wanted to visit here. Okay – go and do that. Now you have got back, back to where you live. You might move to a better house, or you might stay where you are. But what would you involve yourself in? Day to day, in what kind of activities would you be involved if you had absolutely no financial worries? That should give you a strong clue as to the direction your career should be going.

3. What one great thing would you do with your life, if you knew you could not fail? This question comes from Robert Schuller and it is very interesting because many people do know deep in their hearts what they would like to be doing, but they fear failure, they fear rejection, they fear making a fool of themselves. So think very carefully about this question. If you knew you could not fail, what one great thing would you do with your life? Well, have you worked that out? Okay – why don't you do it?

4. If you had six months to live, what would you do in that time? You have been told by the doctor that you are healthy now, but in six months' time he predicts you will have a massive heart attack, you will drop

dead. It will be fairly painless but you will pop off. You will be perfectly healthy up to that point; you can do whatever you want. What would you do in those six months? Who would you meet, who you would visit, where would you go? This in itself will not necessarily help you answer what you should be doing with your life, but it will help you focus in the short term on what is important for you in it.

5. Let's say you are told you have one goal to accomplish in the next thirty days. If it is not accomplished, you will be shot. That's right, you will be shot dead unless you have accomplished this in thirty days. What goal would that be? Do you really believe you could do this in thirty days if you were going to be shot unless it was completed?

6. What activities did you enjoy while you were between the ages of seven and fourteen? This is a very creative age. Children get involved in all sorts of games, pastimes, sports, fun, they have dreams, they have ambitions of what they are going to do. So, between the ages of seven and fourteen, what did you do? What made you happy? What activities were you involved in? What hobbies did you have? What were your dreams then for when you grew up? This is a great clue as to what the inner you is good at. When you are that age, you don't think particularly, "Am I good at this or am I good at that?" – you just participate in activities that come along. So think back. What filled your time, what passed the hours in childhood bliss?

Planes and Magic

Texan Mark Stephenson, as a boy, was fascinated with toy planes. He bought and got as presents every one that could be found, he read books in the library on them, he read how to construct them, how to make them, all about the history of planes, the earliest planes – First World War planes, Second World War planes, fighter planes, jet planes. He built models that could fly. Is it no surprise that when he grew up he became a pilot and went on to own two leasing companies? A man who turned his childhood passion into his livelihood and became a multi-millionaire.

At the age of seven I saw magician Albert le Bas at a birthday party. I was so fascinated that I asked for a magic set for Christmas. We went to the circus that year and saw more magicians. Well, I was hooked. I borrowed some books from the library, and the following Christmas I got an even better magic set. I started doing a few shows for family and a few friends.

Later, on holidays, I met a professional magician who gave me the details of magic supply houses. Subscribing to magicians' magazines and catalogues, I found all sorts of wonderful tricks to buy, make and perform. I started doing some more shows and earning money. I always thought that I would end up being a teacher but by the time I left school and went to college, I was doing a lot of shows. I realised that I would earn more money from magic than as a teacher, so my career went on to being a professional entertainer. I ended up doing ten thousand live shows over twenty-five years! While entertainment is still in my blood and I still regularly perform my mindreading show I also feel the need to cut back and do more training and seminars to help others follow their own intuition, which is one of the reasons I am writing this book.

7. If you retired from your job right now, what would you do with your time? Some people always say, "Well when I get to retirement age I am going to do this, or I am going to do that, or I am going to play more golf, or travel." Why not do this now? Why wait until you are retired? If you are interested in travel, maybe there is a way you might earn money from this. You can

become a tour guide. Couldn't you go and visit places, make contacts, and return later leading groups? A friend from college who was studying art takes people all around Ireland visiting galleries, stately homes and the many little-known locations he has discovered. The clients who come on his tours are absolutely delighted! It would take them years to do the research that he has done.

When you are retired, you might play a lot of golf. Maybe you can find some way of earning money from it now. You don't have to be a professional. Maybe you could open up a golf shop. Perhaps you have some skill or service that you can offer to golf clubs – landscaping or keeping the greens, helping with the management of the place.

Be in the place where your interest lies. If your interest is in golf, be around golfers and golf clubs. If your interest is the cinema, be around cinemas, people who work in cinemas, or the places they make films. A certain teenager wanted nothing more than to make films. What did he do? He went onto the lot of Universal Studios, walked in by the security guard, waved and said hello, and of course after a few days the security guards all recognised him and they thought he worked there. He was in and out all the time. He found a disused trailer and he set up an office there. He was hanging around and eventually became noticed and got to make films. His name is Steven Spielberg!

8. What are you good at? What skills do you have? Make a list of all the things that you can do. It might be driving a car, maybe you have a heavy goods vehicle licence, maybe you are a champion swimmer – maybe you can just swim. Whatever your skills are, whether it is riding a bike, roller skating, trapeze flying, gymnastics – write it down. Look over your life's experiences – places you have been, places you have trav-

elled to and people you have met. See if there is anything there that could help you find and launch a career for yourself.

Dougie Brimson was a hooligan in England in the 1980s when football violence began to take off. He was quite happy to travel around and get involved in any fights that presented themselves. Serious mischief. He says that he had fallen in love with a culture that existed to cause mayhem. Eventually in the mid-1980s he gave it up. He appreciated that he might be seriously hurt. So what did he do from this experience? He went on to become an expert on football hooliganism, realising that the whole thing just amounted to fierce bullying. With his brother he wrote a book on the subject and has since gone on to write three other books selling over a hundred thousand copies. He turned his expertise on football hooliganism into a career as a journalist, author and more recently a consultant.

9. Find a want and fill it. In entrepreneurial and business schools, they teach you to go out, find a need and fill it. This is not great advice. People don't buy what they need. They buy what they want. Nobody needs an expensive car. But people want a BMW or a Mercedes or a Rolls-Royce. You don't need expensive designer clothes, but this is what the multitudes want to wear, and they are quite happy to put their money out and buy the product. So look for a want in the marketplace and see how you can fill it. Look for more on this in Chapter 12.

10. Find a problem and solve it. This is similar to step number 9. You will find as you go along in your day-to-day routine things that niggle you. Mike Dyson was helping his wife vacuum clean one day and became annoyed because as the bag in the machine filled, the suction went down. So he went and invented a vacuum cleaner without the traditional bag, which sold

in Japan at ten times the cost of a regular vacuum cleaner. This success enabled him to set up a factory in England to manufacture the now famous Dyson bagless vacuum cleaner.

11. Draw a large + (plus) sign on a sheet of paper, dividing it into four quarters. In the top left-hand corner, list seven things you absolutely love to do, in work, play, games, recreation, travel. In the top right-hand corner, list all the things you are good at, your talents and skills. Include the things that people tell you that you are good at. Frequently, this will include something you are not even aware you are good at, but others can spot.

    In the bottom left-hand corner, list the seven things you would absolutely have to do for your life to be complete if you discovered you had only five years to live. In the bottom right-hand corner, list the seven things you feel you ought to do. Include any hunches or areas you would like to explore, geographically or intellectually. Things you would do if you had more time.

    Prioritise your lists and select the top three from each. You should see some themes and similarities. From this, you will know what motivates and energises you.

The Blinding Flash

You may find the key comes in a flash. This is what American comedian Dennis Miller has to say about the time his comedic talents dawned on him: *"I was in tenth grade, sitting in a study hall in high school. And sitting next to me was a football player, just about the coolest cat in the school. The seating chart just happened to fall out that way. And I was very small for my age, not particularly adept with women, and not good at sports. And I was always quiet but I always had funny lines in my head. And*

I can remember how this one day I just said what I was thinking, I just spoke the words, and here was this guy looking at me like, 'I can't believe the little gnat said that' – and then he looked at me again and he laughed. He laughed like, 'You're all right, I see you now and I like you.' And God, it was amazing. The feeling of reward. For once I was the experimental rat that got the corn kernels instead of the electric shock. And I went, 'Wait a second, I think he's just laughed at me – I'll do it again.' And I started shooting these lines over at him and he's really laughing and listening to me. God, from that place on ... that was the day."

But I Still Don't Know

Having done all this, if you still are not sure of your life's purpose, here's what to do. Discover your purpose for now. What do you need to do now? It might be to move to a new house, move abroad, raise a child, balance your bank account or get out of debt. Finding this and then following through with it will either reveal to you your life's path or, at the very least, get rid of some of the clutter in your life. You will find out more about this in Chapter 7.

Intelligence versus IQ

Never make the mistake of confusing intelligence with IQ. According to the *New Oxford English Dictionary*, intelligence is the ability to acquire and apply knowledge and skills. IQ (short for Intelligence Quotient) is a number representing a person's reasoning ability measured using problem-solving tests. In other words, IQ measures logical thinking. Intelligence is a way of acting. There are many people with high IQs who are brilliant at what they do. Equally there are many who cannot function very well in the real world. They have high IQs but their lives are a mess. A person of average IQ acting intelligently can achieve far more in life on all levels than a person of high IQ acting stupidly.

You Are More Intelligent Than You Think

Most school subjects come under the headings of either verbal or mathematical intelligence. ***Verbal or linguistic intelligence*** includes speaking a language, writing the language and communicating using the language, getting your point across. ***Mathematical intelligences*** include arithmetic, algebra, some chemistry and some physics.

Between the two, they cover most school studies. Subjects like history and geography require very little comprehension but are largely remembering huge amounts of facts – a verbal intelligence. Subjects like biology are still pretty much memory work – learning and remembering facts. A small amount of comprehension, but mostly remembering facts. Learning foreign languages – verbal intelligence. A lot of people leave school under the impression that they are stupid, dumb, a dunce, because they may not excel at either of these two intelligences.

Dr Howard Gardner in his book *Frames of Mind* found there were many differing intelligences. Psychologists believe that everybody has the potential to operate at genius level in at least one area of their lives.

Physical intelligence. This includes athletes, runners, sportsmen, tennis players and golfers, where the mind and body are perfectly co-ordinated for optimum success. Most athletes will have reached their peak by the age of thirty. Top athletes and sports people in our society earn millions of pounds a year. This comes from prize money, making personal appearances and endorsing other events or products. If they invest this money wisely, they need never work a day for the rest of their lives. But look at them! They don't retire. Staying involved, maybe as a coach, helping others or just playing for the fun of it. They don't stop once they have made the money because they really enjoy what they are doing.

Musical intelligences. If you think back to Beethoven, Mozart – all of the famous composers had incredible musical abilities, operating at genius level. Today there are many people with great musical talents. You might be one of them. You could play a solo instrument or you could be part of a band or group. You could be part of an orchestra, part of an opera company or combining your musical and physical talents you could be a classical, ballet or modern dancer.

Spatial intelligence. People who are very good at working with space and shapes. Architects, for example, and certain disciplines of engineering.

Inter-personal intelligences – includes skilled sales people, negotiators and those very good at teamwork, dealing with and getting on with other people. Good sales people are amongst the top and most highly paid people in our society. Nothing happens in industry without a sale being made. What would be the point of manufacturing goods if they could not be sold? When sales are made, goods get delivered and money comes in, but not until the sale is made. A good salesman is worth a fortune to any company. Good negotiators are also worth their weight in gold. How good are you at dealing with your spouse? How good are you at negotiating a raise? Putting over your point of view?

Intra-personal intelligence – how you deal with yourself, your inner being. How you feel you fit in with the universe and all that is going on around you.

Mechanical intelligence. You might be in your element dismantling machines and putting them back together, fixing cars and engines.

So do realise, whatever field you are in, you may have skills and talents that you are not even aware of. Some people are very good at cooking or gardening. They look on it as a hobby, something they enjoy. But they are not aware they are particularly good at it. You could make a career from something you do in your spare time, which could lead you to lifelong fulfilment and wealth to go with it.

Surely getting paid for what you would be doing for nothing is a sure path for success? Chuck Jones, leaving the US Army after the Second World War, hoped to get his old job back as a janitor in an apartment building. He did not, but as he was looking for another one, somebody offered him a job drawing. Now he had always liked to draw but had never seen any future in it. He went on to become the creator of Bugs Bunny, Daffy Duck and many of the other Warner Brothers cartoons.

Your Winning Streak

You alone have skills and talents that separate you from every other being on the planet. You will also find you are lacking in certain areas. That's okay! Concentrate on what you are good at, your winning streak. You wouldn't bet on a horse you felt might lose so why would you worry about what you can't do? Bet on your strengths. Other people have the skills you lack. Hire them or barter your services. Nobody excels at everything but everyone has the potential to perform at genius level in at least one area.

What do you think about day and night? What do you dream about? What do you spend your spare time doing without thinking about it? People, who do what they love, love what they do. Time flies for them. They work long hours but it is not hard work. It is fun and their peers largely judge them as a standard in their industry, rather than by the amount of money they earn.

Definition of Success: Doing what you would be doing for free but doing it well enough that people will pay you.

"The Secrets of The Universe are locked up in books."

Robert Collier

CHAPTER 4

Becoming an Expert: It's Easier Than You Think

We mentioned earlier the three steps to mastery, purpose, attitude and procedure. Part of the procedure is to become as good as you possibly can, to develop your expertise. If you want to stay in the game you need to keep up with your industry. Keeping abreast of the current trends gives you more options and makes decision making, both logical and intuitive, much easier.

Are you an expert in your field? Do you know everything there is to know about the subject in which you are involved in your career? If not, why not? Do you know how little it takes to become an internationally known expert in your field? You might be quite surprised – just one hour a day. Yes, one hour a day. Get up a bit earlier in the morning. Before you go to work read for one hour on your subject. What should you be reading? For a start all the books you can get your hands on concerning your occupation. All the trade journals pertaining to that subject in your industry. Ask your friends and colleagues to keep an eye out for articles in newspapers or magazines that relate to your field of interest. Reading for one hour a day, for only five days a week – in three years you will become an authority on your subject. In five years you will become an expert. In seven years, you will be regarded as an international expert.

Turn Commuting Time to Profit

In addition, you can speed the time frame along by listening to audio recordings on your subject as you drive to work, as you are exercising or walking around. If you spend half an hour travelling to work every day, and the same again on the return journey, that is one hour per day you can spend with top experts. One hour a day will give you six and a half working weeks per year, practically a university term. Six and a half weeks engrossed in your subject!

Now when you consider your workplace, how many people do you know there who are making any effort at improving their skills and knowledge? They may just learn what they have to know. Imagine if you made the effort of knowing more than the minimum. You would become the acknowledged expert amongst your colleagues. You would be the one to whom they would turn for advice and help. Do you not think that this would get you promotion and therefore enable you to earn a lot more money at what you are doing?

I always listen to tapes whenever I am driving anywhere. In fact, I look forward to long journeys so that I can really get to hear a new set of tapes or re-listen to an old favourite. You will find sources for such tapes listed at the end of the book. I only use the car radio for catching up with news headlines or a particular programme I want to hear. Listening to the endless thump thump of radio music will numb your mind. Other recommended choices while driving are to play your own choice of music or plain silence, giving your subconscious a chance to work. If you are travelling with family or friends, use this time to keep up with news and conversation.

It is not difficult to find an extra hour a day even if you don't get up early. Turn dead time into productive time. Cut down the time you spend reading the newspapers. Any relevant news you can hear in one minute from the radio headlines. Check what you need to know from the papers and don't be distracted by interesting but irrelevant stories. Eliminate couch potato TV time. Video record any television programmes you want to see and watch them at your convenience. You can then fast forward through the ads with your remote control. I generally purchase only one newspaper a week, usually a weekend one that covers the past seven days.

If you find difficulty in obtaining suitable recordings to listen to, select relevant passages from books or magazines and record these yourself onto tape. It is not necessary to record the whole book, just the points or passages you feel are most useful and worth recalling. The combination of reading and listening will launch you into the stratosphere of success, knowledge and expertise in your field. The more you listen to the cassette, the more the points will reinforce themselves onto your subconscious mind.

Repeated listening has further benefits. While listening to an idea, your mind goes off on tangents of thoughts and possibilities and later you go back to consciously listening to the tape. So you will miss something. I have listened to some cassettes ten and twelve times and amazed myself at finding ideas I had missed before. Also some points that have little relevance now may well be very relevant in six or twelve months' time. Your circumstances, needs and wants will have changed.

Many industries have major national and international conventions and frequently the talks or lectures at these are recorded. If these interest you, buy as many of them as possible. This is especially useful if you cannot get to that particular convention. Every year the American National Speakers Association have three major get-togethers. All the talks and workshop groups are recorded, some on video, all on audio. So, if I cannot get to one of these conventions it is wonderful for me to be able, at a very reasonable cost, to buy the tapes and listen at my leisure.

Reading for one hour a day and listening to tapes will make you an acknowledged expert in your field, and I give it my highest and most earnest recommendation.

> ***"Learn to work harder on yourself than you do on your job. If you work hard on your job you will earn a living. If you work hard on yourself you will make a fortune."* Jim Rohn.**

How To Become An Instant Authority

Let us say you are a girl who has spotted a handsome guy at the office. You would like to get to know him better. You hear his passion is motorbikes. You know absolutely nothing about them but it strikes you that some information on the subject would break the ice. Wouldn't you like to be able to talk to him with knowledge and authority? As most girls know nothing about bikes where would you start? The easiest and simplest way is to buy a couple of current bike magazines at the local newsagent. Spend an hour with them, read the reviews, study the ads and find out what the current trends are. If you know what model he rides, see if there is anything about it. Perhaps it has a special gizmo that allows it go into overdrive.

Bump into him when he is with his bike. Pay him some compliment about it. You can drop a couple of lines about the trends in bikes, or about some potential government legislation about to be introduced concerning bikes. Ask if his bike has the special overdrive gizmo. He will be taken aback and think you are the most interesting girl he has ever met. You will really impress him.

You can use this technique with any subject. Before I bought a computer I purchased a few computer magazines. I quickly learned all I needed to know to make a suitable buying decision.

Before I learnt to scuba dive I did the same with a couple of diving magazines. I learnt the current trends, the better diving spots around the world and the latest technical advances. I was even able to tell the instructor something he didn't know. Simply by spending an hour with a couple of magazines you will be able to talk with confidence on practically any area of interest.

Barristers use similar techniques for court cases. They frequently must have enough in-depth knowledge of a subject to be able to cross-examine expert witnesses.

Shortening the Learning Curve

It goes without saying that studying alone will only make you an academic expert. You need plenty of hands-on experience in the field. If you were to ask me how to become an entertainer I would tell you to get in front of as many audiences as possible. No amount of study is as good a teacher as actually doing it. You won't be great at the beginning but like the little guy in the cartoon at the start of this chapter you will make measurable progress if you take it one step at a time. Mixing the hands-on experience with reading and listening will shorten your learning curve by years.

The other trick in becoming an expert is to stick with

a narrow field of interest – your niche. Studying in too many areas diffuses your main skill and you will be eminently suitable for pub quizzes and TV game shows but little else. You want to be the expert in your field. When oil wells catch fire there is one man on top of everyone's list: Red Adair. That's who you want to be in your area.

Achieving Pre-Eminence in Your Field

Economists and planners see, use and work with statistics, with spreadsheets, graphs and data research. Logical things. Things you can measure. Scientists want experiments with consistent results. They must know that when you start cause A, result B will follow. This is one of the laws of the universe – cause and effect.

What happens though when you add the human element?

Let's look at a drug company testing a new product. Some of the tablets are the real thing and others are placebos, sugar sweets with no active ingredients. During the test period the doctors administering these do not know themselves which are the drugs and which are the sweets. If they did, they might involuntarily give that information away to the patient, or the patient might intuitively pick it up from the doctor's body language. There are strong psychological forces at work here. The patient believes he is taking a new drug. His belief system that the drug will be of benefit takes over, and this in itself may well lead to a cure. Now this belief cannot be measured. In fact, the patient may not be consciously aware of it. Likewise, when doing research, things like the states of joy, happiness, fear or anger are not taken into account. They cannot be measured. This is something that is pretty much ignored in business. People are not the same all of the time. Their moods vary. So where is this leading us?

In business you are dealing with other human beings. They, like you, have wants, needs, cares, desires, the need to be loved, to belong and to have friends. Empathy is needed with your customer. Put yourself in your customer's position and ask yourself these five questions:

1. If I were on the receiving end, why would I want this?
2. Why would I want this now?
3. What's in it for me?
4. How will this product or service make me feel better about my family, my business, my life and myself?
5. Why is this better than what I am already doing?

Bear this in mind. Most business people fall in love with their product instead of their prospect. That is, they fall in love with what they are selling instead of their customer. This is important in all areas of your life, not just in your business dealings. If you want your son to do something, you are more interested in what you want done than in him. So put yourself in his position and give him a motivation to do what it is you want done.

Have you ever noticed how so many advertisements in magazines tell you how wonderful they and their product are? "Jones and Son, we sell gizmos and give first-class quality and service." A hundred other ads say similar uninteresting things. You need to tell the customer what you will do for him. What are the benefits for him?

Imagine an ad in the Yellow Pages for Jones & Son Plumbers saying "WE SHOW UP". Wouldn't you phone them first? They would make a fortune. They are putting you first. So do the same for your customer.

Remember, everything you will ever achieve in life comes from dealing with and through other people. That is a sobering thought. In business you are working with three sets of people. The first set is obviously your customer and indeed without your customer buying something or some transaction going on, nothing really happens. As we discussed earlier, the whole world of commerce and business happens when sales are made.

So you have to sell to these customers, but you also

have to sell your vision and your point of view to the people who supply you in your business. These you want to keep "onside", so that they want the best for you and ultimately what is best for your customer. And it helps enormously if you make the effort to see things from your suppliers' point of view and help them along. The more you help your supplier, the more your supplier will be in the right frame of mind to help you, because the more you earn and the more business you do, the more business he does.

The third set is your fellow team members, your coworkers – maybe you call them your employees or your boss or whatever. You may have to "sell" your point of view, your ideas, to make sure everyone sees the goalposts and is moving in the right direction. You need to understand in a very compassionate and respectful way how the others in the transaction feel and view the situation.

The Weekly Shopper Who Spends £25,000

Remember in Chapter 1 we spoke about looking at the tree and how it was much more than it first appeared? Whatever you are working on, don't just concentrate on the deal at hand now. You never know where one transaction may lead. Most people in business see a transaction as just that – a single transaction. But that client may come back and buy from you for many years down the road.

A new customer with a family walking into a supermarket may spend £100 a week on groceries. That is £5,000 a year. If a family lives in that area for five years, that is £25,000 they will spend with you. If you do your very utmost, as the supermarket owner or worker to put yourself in your customer's position and do everything to make things easier, to help her make better decisions and give her good service, she will want to come back again and again. Alienating her by doing things that you want to do, as opposed to things the customer might want to do is actually turning away £25,000 worth of business. Do that to enough customers and you certainly have problems. Always take a few moments to see the bigger picture.

A vs. B

Becoming an expert will put you way ahead of the pack. Your decision making will be easier as you will have more options available to you. For example options A and B are available and a decision has to be made. But you have been keeping up to date and are aware that new technology will make option A obsolete within a year. Your decision now is whether to go for B or wait, if you have time, and fully investigate the new technology. By not going with A you are saving your company a lot of money.

Even if A and B appear to be the only options, allow yourself to intuitively feel the outcome of each. See yourself in the future having gone with option A. How does it feel? Are you happy? Are those around you happy? Does it feel right? Repeat this with option B. Which is the better outcome? Which feels best?

> ***"If you are not investing at least 10% of your gross income (and preferably of your desired income) in your knowledge, know-how, training and conditioning, via books, tapes, newsletters, seminars, coaching and consulting, I think you are incapable of sustaining high performance."***
> **Dan Kennedy**

"I always wanted to be somebody but I should have been more specific."
Erma Bombeck

CHAPTER 5

Creating Your Own World

One of the first things you learn in school and the foundation of most religions is that "God made the world". But God did not create your world. You have within you the godlike ability to create your own world. From pure thought you can dream up services, products or systems. Sure, you don't think up a new house and there it is, but you can dream up the kind of house you want, describe it to an architect, have the plans drawn up and have it built. As I am writing this, a good friend of mine is doing just that. He conceived the idea for the kind of house he wanted and is well on his way to having it created. This book came from an idea. Yes, it's taking time to bring it all together. But I created it in my mind first.

What is even more exciting is that you can create your own lifestyle, your whole existence, not just the things in it. You can create your own life's journey. The alternative is to become a part of someone else's – and that's a spooky thought.

Dream up the lifestyle you want for yourself. Write it down and visualise it clearly. Decide that you really want it, and then work out how to bring it into reality. Being human, that will take longer. For the moment, just be aware that you have the ability to create your own world and you have the lead part.

When faced with a problem, people regularly feel they have to compete with others for a share of the pie. This is very narrow thinking. One good option is to work with others in your field to create a bigger pie. Cavett Robert, founder of the National Speakers Association, said speakers should stop competing for the available work. By working together, they could build a bigger pie and each person have a bigger share of it.

An even better option is to create a new pie, your pie. Three times in my business life I have come up against someone who was battling for a share of my pie. I realised that competing was taking up lots of time and leading me nowhere. I analysed the situation and changed course, creating something new for my product in the marketplace. Not only did I grow, I created better value for my customers, more profit for me and a pie that was much more difficult for a competitor to attack. It took me to a higher level. The moral is "create", don't "compete".

Become Yourself

Cary Grant said, "I played Cary Grant so often, I eventually became him." Miles Davis, jazz trumpeter, said, "Sometimes you have to practice a lot to sound like yourself." A few years before he died, Jimmy Stewart was being interviewed. "Mr Stewart, you have made lots of movies, do you think you will ever act again?" "I'm acting now." This doesn't mean that Jimmy Stewart was not being true to himself. He was being more himself than most people are. He had decided who he wanted to be and polished the parts of his personality that were congruent with that. He became himself. These men concentrated on polishing their better points.

Many celebrities and would-be actors try to be something they are not. As they are going against the grain, this leads to inner stress and turmoil, often leading to drink and drug abuse.

Personal injury solicitor John Schütte noticed that some of his clients were slow to settle their claims cases. It was not that they wanted more money. They were just delaying settling the case. He was puzzled until it dawned on him with a blinding flash of the obvious. They weren't settling their cases because they enjoyed the attention they were receiving. Their family, friends and neighbours were paying more attention than they had ever paid before. Doctors, solicitors, barristers, actuaries were contacting them. They felt so important. They had a purpose in life. Deep down was the realisation that this would all end when the case was settled. Instead of allowing the circumstance of an accident to bring attention to them, with only a little thought and some effort, they could create a useful role for themselves or develop a service that would bring them to the notice of others in their community, especially after they had received their settlement money. They, like you, already have the essentials to design their own destiny.

Every child starts life with a highly creative nature, exploring, questioning, learning, and as they grow older it is repressed as the child is made to conform. As a boy, Peter Ustinov's parents received a school report card with the note: "He shows great originality which must be curbed at all cost."

The Key to Creativity

The key to creativity is stimulation. This is vitally important for both adults and children. After the fall of communism Romanian babies adopted by European families did not react to hands-on stimulation such as hugging or cuddling. They had no close physical contact with other humans in the orphanages. So the touching and holding, the bonding stimuli, were never bridged with the brain. When the babies were eventually adopted, it was too late.

In an experiment with kittens, scientists kept a couple of them blindfolded for six months after their eyes opened (which they do ten days after birth). Even though the eyes of the cats were physically perfect, they remained blind because the early necessary stimuli with the synapses of the brain had not been initiated and linked.

Powerful Problem Blasters

We are now going to look at some ways of stimulating creativity. While they appear logical, and start out that way, their true purpose is to get the subconscious flowing.

The Earl Nightingale Twenty-Answer Method

First thing in the morning Earl Nightingale would get a pad of paper and on top of the first page write down a question or problem. He would then write twenty answers to this question underneath. Now, the first ten answers usually come easily – the last ten can be much more difficult, particularly the last three or four. Many of these answers would have little merit. But usually there would be one or two that would be absolutely brilliant, and would lead him off in other fields, and other lucrative areas.

Some of the ways of finding answers:

You might decide that one of your answers was "make it bigger", so you might then write down the opposite "make it smaller". Make it wider, make it shorter. So look down the answers you have written and then write the opposite to that, or turn the answer inside out. We are just looking for answers. As you write them down, don't worry about how good or bad they are, just write until you get to twenty answers. Remember, the trick is to get the subconscious mind flowing.

Another variation of this method is to just write down five answers per day to the same question. Five answers per day for a week, and sooner or later, possibly after just a few days, the answer will come to you so clearly, so startlingly and with such clarity that you will be astonished that you could think up such an amazingly simple answer.

Imitate and Recreate

> ***"Ordinary people learn from experience, wise people learn from the experience of others."***

A very interesting way of solving a problem is to actually copy someone who has been there before you, somebody who has had the same problem. See what they did, how they solved it, and how they came to the conclusions that they did. Then adapt their solution to your problem. This person may have even written a book about it.

If you were going to start up a car company, you would be well off reading the books by Lee Iacocca on how he turned around the Chrysler Corporation.

Reading the biographies and autobiographies of successful people will give you amazing insights into how they think and how they solved problems. You will always find something that will be useful and of great benefit to you. I recommend that you keep a notebook or journal for ideas that you find. Don't take shorthand notes, but make a reasonably detailed account because you may not come back and re-read it for a few years. If you make just little shorthand notes, you won't have the foggiest notion of what it was about. The more detailed explanation in your journal the better. Use the creative ideas of others and use your own creativity to adapt their solutions to your problems.

Thomas Edison's Method

Thomas Alva Edison, who invented many things including the electric light bulb still used today, was renowned for how little sleep he got each night. What he used to do during the day was take catnaps. If he had a problem on his mind, or had reached a dead end, he would relax back on his workbench, with a couple of steel nuts clenched in his fist. Relaxing with the problem on his mind he would drift off to sleep. His hand would drop releasing the nuts to clatter on the floor. The noise would awaken him and he would get back to work advancing with a new perspective to the problem.

The Mastermind Group

In his classic book *Think and Grow Rich*, Napoleon Hill puts great emphasis on "The Mastermind Group" as a tremendously effective path to creative problem solving.

Assemble a group of friends who have similar ambitions and ideas of success as yourself. Avoid people with little or no ambition. They should be from differing backgrounds and industries. Perhaps a doctor, a lawyer, a builder, a storeowner, a football coach and a mechanic. The main thing is different business backgrounds. A group from the same industry will have a narrow focus. Bringing together different industrial outlooks results in a synergy of ideas and creativity that is astonishing. Somebody not familiar with your work can bring a new fresh perspective to a problem that may have bothered you for years.

You must all commit to meet regularly, if possible once a week. You can meet for breakfast, lunch, dinner or perhaps a Saturday morning mastermind get-together. Give yourselves a name like "The Millionaire's Club", or "The Omega Group". A Monday morning breakfast meeting will give a great boost to your week.

The Imaginary Mastermind Group

So you like the idea of the Mastermind group but don't know enough like-minded achievers to get together on a regular basis. At least you don't know them *yet*. Use this method, which also works well in conjunction with the real mastermind group.

You develop your imaginary group of "Master Minds." In your own private group you can have anyone you want, living or dead, anyone from history or anyone living you admire. Select six to eight such individuals. You might choose Alexander the Great, Socrates, Mohammed Ali, Albert Einstein, Margaret Thatcher, P.T. Barnum and Florence Nightingale. You should know at least a little about each of them and know you would value their advice. A visit to the reference section of your public library will yield information on them.

In your mind's eye visualise them all sitting around a table or relaxing at your home. Pose your question and ask each for his (or her) input. This may sound daft to you but it is an exciting process. You are tapping into the intuitive minds of not only yourself but some of the greatest minds who ever lived. Six to eight different perspectives on your problem should reveal the solution to you.

The Self-Made Millionaire's Method

Benjamin Franklin, the first ever American self-made millionaire, developed this method of problem solving. It works well when your answer is either "yes" or "no". Write your question on the top of a sheet of paper. Now draw a vertical line down the middle of the page, dividing it into two equal sides. On top of the left side write the word "for" and on top of the right side "against".

In the left-hand column under "for" write all the reasons you can think in favour. In the right-hand column write all the reasons against. Make sure you list all the reasons. Before you get into bed that night look over the page and re-read all the reasons listed. If any more come to mind, jot them down in the appropriate column. Ask yourself the question and tell yourself you need the answer when you wake up in the morning. The answer should be a definite "yes" or "no". If for some reason you are still not sure assume the answer is "no". Once you have your decision do not logically second-guess yourself. Run with it.

I have seen another way of using the Franklin technique. Having listed all your reasons you give them points out of three. A good reason will merit 3 points, an average one, 2 points, and a poor one, 1 point. Add up all the points for each column. Whichever side "for" or "against" gets the highest points you go with. The decision is made. I do not like this version, as it is too logical and too prone to error. It is much better to "sleep on it".

The Letting-Go Technique

Something has been worrying or bothering you, or you have been working away at a problem and you can't really make any progress. Well, you just simply "let it go". That's all – simply let it go. Stop thinking about it and get yourself involved in something else. Sooner or later, the answer will come to you. But before you let it go, actually tell your subconscious mind that you want the answer to the problem.

A ham radio operator cannot receive when he is broadcasting. He can only receive from what is out there when he is in receptive mode. This is the equivalent of hearing from your subconscious. You may be driving down the road, you may be washing the dishes, but you will be involved in some activity that has nothing to do with the problem, and suddenly the answer will come to you in a blinding flash. You may have had this experience already in your life, and the answer will come with such clarity that you will be astonished.

Now you must go and act on that answer. Otherwise when you use this technique at a later date, your intuitive self may say, "Well look, the last time he never bothered, so why should I make an effort now?"

Another time the answer may come is in the middle of the night. You will wake up with the solution and you will be sitting there marvelling at how wonderful the answer is, and how clever you are at thinking it up! You will say, "Great – I will remember that when I wake up in the morning." Now here is the snag and the catch. You won't remember it in the morning. This I promise you! You will recall having the solution; you will recall it being brilliant; but you will have forgotten what it was. You must get up and write it down. Have a small Dictaphone or a pen and paper beside your bed. And do make detailed notes. Two or three words may mean nothing later.

The Saddam Hussein Idea Generation Method (not recommended)

General Norman Schwarzkopf tells how Saddam Hussein generates ideas. Before the Gulf War, the situation between the US and Iraq was extremely tense. Saddam Hussein called all his generals and aides together with a view of brainstorming ideas to find a solution that would avoid war.

There was a dearth of suggestions. A long-time close friend of the Iraqi leader broke the silence. He suggested, as diplomatically and tactfully as possible, that the scenario had become a spitting contest between Saddam Hussein and George Bush. Emotions, egos and saving face were all involved. To save Iraq from the seemingly inevitable impending war, if Saddam were to temporarily step down as president, a puppet president could take over. Saddam would be the real leader in the background, and later, when the situation calmed down, he could take over again as president. Taking out his gun Saddam shot the man dead. He turned to the group, "Who else has an idea?"

"A person's chances for success tend to increase the more he's out of step with the dictates of 'conventional wisdom'." **Robert Ringer**

CHAPTER 6

The Other Side of the Mirror

This is the best method I know for finding new ways of doing things, discovering greatness, developing your career, achieving peace of mind, acquiring wealth, and ending up with a deep feeling of accomplishment.

Occasionally, something happens unexpectedly, throwing you off course or in a totally different direction. It is as if one door has closed and another door could well open. It could be the death of a friend or a family member, government legislation changing the nature of your business, an enemy doing you a mischief. Perhaps you see a major problem in your way or in the way of others close to you. Maybe it is a natural disaster. Every setback is a marker for even greater triumph. It all depends on your attitude. Are you prepared to wallow in self-pity or turn the setback inside out into glorious accomplishment? When you see a problem, do you see a setback, a challenge or an opportunity?

The Story of Two Men

Twin boys were born to a family. The mother was a good woman doing her best for them. The father was a smoker and a heavy drinker; he gambled, got involved in drugs and petty crime. He was regularly in and out of prison. He couldn't hold a job. He developed violent tendencies and was killed in a street fight. The boys grew up. One never touched a drink, cigarettes or drugs. He studied hard and developed a promising career. The other took after his father and ended up in prison. They were both asked the same question. "Why do you think you are in the situation you are in?" They each answered with the same words – "What would you expect with a father like mine?"

The Benefit from a Cancelled Flight

A few years ago I was travelling to London from Dublin. I was catching the last flight out on Friday evening for a conference that was being held on Saturday and Sunday. Arriving at the airport I was told that the flight had been cancelled because there was a problem with the plane, and that they would put me out on the next flight, which was six-thirty on the Saturday morning.

I knew in my heart and soul with that news that I was not going to be flying out on the Friday night and I would have to wait until first thing Saturday morning. But I decided to press my luck and see where it would lead. At the very least, I was still going to be travelling the following morning at six-thirty.

I said to the girl behind the desk "That's okay, but they have small private companies here at the airport that lease out private jets to businessmen. There are a few other passengers here waiting to fly off, so why don't you hire one of those private jets and we will be sure to get to London this evening."

She went off to talk to the manager. Returning she said that the manager had offered to put everybody up in a nearby hotel and throw in dinner! This pleased the other passengers no end as they had been prepared to walk away with empty hands. Since I lived reasonably close to the airport, I asked how much the hotel would cost for the night. About £90 with dinner. So I said well, I live nearby and it is easy enough for me to get out to the airport in the morning. The return flight I am paying for is £69, so if you are prepared to give me a free return flight at a later date, I would be happy to accept that instead of staying at the hotel. Again she consulted and said yes, the manager agrees to that! The other passengers had a night in a hotel with dinner and I had a free flight at a later date.

The free flight came simply by looking for an opportunity where there was a setback. If you end up missing a flight, or are considerably delayed, why not look for opportunity where you are. The time could yield an article for a trade publication or a newspaper item about your business. You could look up the local Yellow Pages and make a business contact – you never know where that might lead.

A friend of mine was stuck at an airport for three hours. The next flight out was not going to be until ten at night, so he looked around. Sitting nearby was a girl from the same flight about his own age, and he thought she looked interesting, so he went over and invited her to dinner. They did indeed go and have an enjoyable meal. Now nothing further came from this. They have not seen or spoken to each other since, but it did pass what was a very pleasant three hours!

The Technique

The technique is to look at the problem and imagine the opposite on the other side of a mirror, not your reflection in the mirror, but the reflection of the problem in the mirror: 99.9 times of out 100 you will find something to your advantage. Something you may never have found otherwise. It may even completely change your life for the better. What can you create from this opportunity?

The Salesman's Secret

A photocopy machine salesman had a very good system for getting leads. These would be potential customers. He found that for every hundred good leads he got, he could actually sell five machines. These were at the more expensive end of the market. So for every hundred leads he got, he sold five and there were ninety-five people who were still interested, but not in his particular brand. He did something that most people would never even dream of. He contacted one of his competitors and he offered them the ninety-five leads he was not able to sell to. The deal was that the competitor would aim to sell to them. The salesman would get a percentage of these profits. He ended up making more money from the leads he didn't sell than from the leads he did! He was happy, the customers were happy and his competitor was happy. He created a bigger market. Not by competing, but by creating – by looking for an opportunity on the other side of the mirror.

How Do You View Events?

"It was the best of times; it was the worst of times." Is it always the best of times or is it always the worst? The times actually don't care. They are neutral. They will go on doing their own thing in their own way as they have done since the beginning of time. Right until the end of time. The times are quite perfect and are oblivious to everything else. They just are. It is our perceptions of them that vary. "Nothing is either good or bad, but thinking makes it so," said Shakespeare. Where some see danger, death and closed doors, others see growth, life and golden opportunity.

In the 1950s a British shoe manufacturer, acting on a hunch, sent one of his top salesmen to Africa. His brief was to assess the market, find an importer and distributor based locally, and order the first shipment. After three days he reported to the office – "Absolutely useless. Am coming back home. Nobody here wears shoes. It's a total waste of time." The shoe manufacturer was disappointed but still felt that there must be some opening in the marketplace somewhere. Deciding to give it another shot, he sent another salesman. After two days came the response: "Send two containers of shoes. Nobody here has any. We have the market to ourselves."

The Parable of the Bricklayers

Imagine you are the foreman of a building site and you have three bricklayers, each about the same age, height and build. You might be surprised at the responses you get from this simple question. "What are you doing?" The first says, "I am laying bricks." The second says, "I am earning £10 an hour." The third says, "I am building a house." Interesting, isn't it? On the face of it, all things are equal and yet you have three different attitudes from three people to the exact same task.

The Wily Politician

In the State of Mississippi, in the old Bible belt, where prohibition still had its strongest citadel, there's a story of an incident that illustrates a point. Some years ago the editor of the *Macon Beacon*, a little country paper, asked a local politician, during a campaign, how he stood on the whiskey question. What a dreadful thing to do to anyone in the State of Mississippi who is running for office! You see, you are damned if you do, and damned if you don't. If you say, "I am for whiskey," you will get half of the votes and you will lose half. If you say, "I am against whiskey," you will lose half and get half. And if there are over two in the race, you are in trouble.

But this local politician acquitted himself admirably. This is what he wrote back to the paper:

"Sir, I had not planned to discuss this controversial question at this time but far be it for me to sidestep any issue, regardless of the nature and regardless of the result. But I want to be sure I understand you now, sir. If when you say whiskey, you mean that devil's brew, that poison scourge, that bloody monster that defies cogent reasoning, creates misery and poverty, takes the very bread out of the mouth of babes, if when you say whiskey if you mean that vile drink that topples the Christian man and woman from the pinnacles of righteous and gracious living into the bottomless pit of despair, deprivation, shame, hopelessness and helplessness, destroys homes, creates orphans and depraves the community in general, sir, if that is what you mean by whiskey, I want you to put in your paper I promise my constituents if I am elected I will fight to destroy this demon with all the strength I possess.

"But, if on the other hand, when you say whiskey, if you mean that oil of conversation, if you mean that philosophical wine and ale that's consumed when good fellows get together, puts a song in their heart, laughter in their soul, warm contentment in their eyes, sir, if you mean that medicinal spirit that puts a spring in the old man's step on a frosty morning, if you mean that nectar of the gods, the sale of which puts untold millions in our treasury, tends to the care for our orphan children, the blind and the deaf, the halt and the maimed, aged and infirm, builds great highways, schools, hospitals, makes this world a better place in which to live, now sir if that's what you mean by whiskey, I want you to put in your paper I promise my constituents if I am elected I will fight to protect this essence of divinity with all the strength I possess."

And then he added the crowning climax, the capstone of it all. He said, "Sir, now that I have answered your query without equivocation I hope you will in good conscience put in your paper that I am a man with the courage of my convictions. This is my stand, I will not compromise, this is my stand!"

What Would You Have Seen?

A couple of years after leaving school I was shopping in Dublin City Centre. Activity in a crowd attracted my attention. I went over to have a look. In the centre was a tall man wearing clothes that were once fashionable and good quality. He was making a series of noises, mimicking birds and animals. You could visualise all the birds he conjured up purely by the sounds he made. Likewise you could see the small animals, the mouse and the yapping dog. I was truly enthralled, even though I knew how he did it.

I had seen the device he used advertised in mail-order catalogues as the "bird warbler" or "ventrillo", a small reed-like device inserted in the mouth behind the front teeth which whistled when air passed through it. Depending on the force of air and the position of the tongue and lips, you could mimic birds and small animals, and this guy was brilliant.

Eventually he showed the crowd how it worked and he was selling the device and a little book of instructions for a small sum. As I said, I was really enthralled by his performance, excited by his ability to entertain, and a little in awe of his skill. I looked up and standing close by me, also watching the demonstration, was one of my old teachers from school. "What do you think?" I asked. "It is pitiful to see someone reduced so low to working on the streets," he said.

Again the two sides of the mirror. While I saw fun, entertainment, skill, the freedom to earning a living as you wished, he saw poverty, loss and shame.

Heaven and Hell: What's the Difference?

A man was given the opportunity to visit both heaven and hell. The trip started with the descent to hell and looking around he found a great banquet table laid out. There was plenty of food and drink and everybody was sitting around, glum, gloomy, depressed and definitely not enjoying themselves.

Upon going up to heaven, he found exactly the same situation. Food, drink, everything was there, and yet all those sitting around the table were happy, relaxed, enjoying themselves, laughing away. He thought, "How could this be?" and looked closer. Then he remembered that the people in hell had strapped to their right arm a knife, on their left arm a fork. The knives and forks were three feet long, so they could not reach down, cut their food, pick it up or eat it. It was just impossible from the length of the cutlery, but the people in heaven were in exactly the same position. They had long knives and forks strapped on their hands and arms, but the difference was that the people in heaven were using their knives and forks to feed the people sitting at the table opposite them.

By helping others, they could be helped themselves. In hell, nobody was prepared to help anybody. In heaven, by helping others they were able to have a great time.

Plague: Death or Renewal?

The Black Plague. In the 1300s Europe was ravaged by the bubonic plague, also known as the Black Death. Over one-third of the population was wiped out.

I expect you recall the nursery rhyme, "Ring a ring of roses, a pocket full of posies, atishoo, atishoo, we all fall down." The first symptoms were reddish rings that appeared on the skin, followed by violent sneezing, before the victim fell down dead. It was truly a horrendous time and the plague was not choosy as to whom it took as a victim. Rich or poor, nobleman or peasant, priest or craftsman. Can you imagine the effect if a similar plague hit today? One-third of all the people you know wiped out. Gruesome thought, isn't it?

But what of the other side of the mirror? Did it have a positive effect on the population? Obviously not for those who died!

Well, people started to live outside the feudal walls of cities. They began to enjoy themselves more and the tradition of fairs and fetes sprang up. Because of inheritances from those who died, people were wealthier than they had ever been before. With the shortage of labourers, workers could and did charge more for their work. It began to dawn on people that they could shake off the yoke of oppression of the Dark Ages. Rather than accept their lot, people began to question the accepted norms and to think for themselves. The church's reaction was to turn back the clock and establish the Inquisition, to no avail. People had started to think for themselves and a mind once stretched will never go back to the same condition. The people realised that there was more to life than working to get into the next one. This spark of enlightenment, in spite of the inquisition, led to the Renaissance and the age of discovery.

So was the bubonic plague good, bad or neutral? It closed the door to the Dark Ages and opened the door to the Renaissance. What do you think?

The Phoenix

The messenger called to Thomas Edison's house. "The factory is on fire!" Edison, one of the world's greatest inventors, hurried down to see his factory totally gutted. One of his employees, with tears in his eyes, implored, "What will we do, what will we do, it is the most awful thing that could have happened." "No," said Edison, "it is a blessing. We have burned all our mistakes. Tomorrow we will start afresh."

Things That Go Bang

The early 1860s saw much experimenting with nitroglycerine. Made from nitric acid and glycerine, it was far more powerful than gunpowder. It did have one major drawback. Being very volatile, it could explode easily and with no warning, usually blasting those nearby through the door into the eternity that was just outside, and far closer than many of us realise. If you were able to get it outside the laboratory, you needed glass containers as the acid corroded metal. Even a small shake could set off the explosive.

Alfred Nobel started experimenting with nitro-glycerine. He saw great potential in mining, tunnelling, building roads and railroads with the product. So he resolved to make it safe to handle. After much trial and error, he settled on finely ground sawdust, which absorbed the nitroglycerine. By packaging it in long cylindrical containers, it was perfect to fit into the holes drilled in rock for tunnelling and mining. He called it dynamite. He set up factories all over the world and, as a result, became a very wealthy man. Soon, others started to use his invention for destruction, war and killing. What he intended as a positive contribution to the world was now being used as a negative one. He did not want to be remembered for the negative effects. Looking to see the positive side, he set up the Nobel Foundation, which makes awards for contributors to the fields of physics, chemistry, literature, medicine and peace.

Would You Have Seen the Potential Genius?

In her book, *Revolution from Within: A Book of Self-Esteem*, Gloria Steinem tells the story of the Royal Knights of Harlem. Spanish Harlem, around the area of East 101st Street in New York, is similar in many ways to a third world country. Mortality rates are high, and life is very tough for the people who live there. Another major disadvantage is that most of the children who live there do not speak English.

Bill Hall, a teacher in the local high school, was looking for a way to motivate some of the students, and he started a chess club. After some initial excitement, the club dwindled to twelve members. These teenage boys started to learn chess and their command of the English language grew also. As their chess skills developed they began to play other schools in the area and won the games. Their self-confidence grew, and Bill Hall started to give each boy responsibilities for the organization of transportation to matches and in coaching some of the others. Again, their self-confidence continued to improve. Success in the State finals in Syracuse, New York, led to the Junior High School Finals in California. Only playing chess for a few months, they finished seventeenth out of the 109 teams. An invitation followed to travel to Russia for the Scholastic Chess Friendship games. They put Spanish Harlem and their school on the map.

Eventually, with career plans that included law, accounting, teaching and computer sciences – they had futures they would not have thought possible before, their self-image and self-confidence had increased exponentially. "What were you doing?" they were asked, "before Bill Hall and chess playing came into your lives?" "Hanging out in the street and feeling pretty awful," said one boy now planning to become a lawyer. "Taking lunch money from younger kids and a few drugs now and then," said another. "What made the difference?" they were asked. "Not until Mr Hall thought we were smart," explained one, "and then we were."

The Birth of a Negotiator

American TV talk show host Larry King tells of a textbook use of the mirror technique. In high school Larry and two friends, Herb Cohen and Brazzie Albate, had a classmate who developed tuberculosis. His family quickly moved from

New York to Arizona for the warmer climate. The family asked Larry and his pals to notify the school authorities.

With all the mischievousness of teenagers, they decided to tell the school the boy had died, collect money for flowers and instead use it for burgers and cola. The scheme took off and the three "musketeers" were able to enjoy considerable helpings of their favourite snack foods.

The principal decided to award a prize in memory of the deceased boy, to that year's outstanding student. On the first day of the following term, in the school auditorium, as the memorial award was about to be made, the now recovered "deceased" student turned up. You can imagine the pandemonium that ensued.

The three boys were ordered to the principal's office and told they were being expelled – and would never graduate. While Larry and Brazzie contemplated the bleak life ahead of them, Herb looked to the other side of the mirror. He turned to the principal, "We may not graduate, but you will surely lose your job. You took the word of three teenagers who have been in trouble before. There will be a hearing. We may be out of school but you will be out of work ... Why don't we forget the whole thing?" The principal thought for a few moments and agreed. The boys stayed on in school and graduated. Herb Cohen went on to develop a career in negotiating and wrote the book *You Can Negotiate Anything*.

The Ping-Pong Ball

I hold up a ping-pong ball and I ask you what colour is it? White, you answer. No, I say, it's black. Try again. You look again; no it's definitely white. No, I say, it's black. You look again. Well, it definitely looks white and I say well, it's definitely black. I turn the ball around and you see it's painted white on your side and black on my side. Two people can come from two different perspectives and both can be right.

WOW!

Rob Gilbert, editor of *Bits & Pieces* contributes this story:

Last spring I was walking in a park. A short distance ahead of me was a mom and her three-year-old daughter. The little girl was holding on to a string that was attached to a helium balloon.

All of a sudden, a sharp gust of wind took the balloon from the little girl. I braced myself for some screaming and crying.

But, no! As the little girl turned to watch her balloon go skyward, she gleefully shouted out, "Wow!"

I didn't realise it at that moment, but that little girl taught me something.

Later that day, I received a phone call from a person with news of an unexpected problem. I felt like responding with "Oh no, what should we do?" But remembering that little girl, I found myself saying, "Wow, that's interesting! How can I help you?"

One thing for sure – life's always going to keep us off balance with its unexpected problems. That's a given. What's not preordained is our response. We can choose to be frustrated or fascinated.

No matter what the situation, a fascinated "Wow!" will always beat a frustrated "Oh, no."

So the next time you experience one of life's unexpected gusts, remember that little girl and make it a "Wow!" experience. The "Wow!" response always works.

"History, despite its wrench and pain, cannot be unlived. But if faced with courage, need not be lived again."
Maya Angelou, poet.

CHAPTER 7

Little Leaks That Keep Men Poor

Perhaps the ancient astrologers were right. Certain events do seem to affect our lives. Strange things do happen when there is a full moon. If the sun and the moon affect the oceans causing tides isn't it logical that we humans, who are largely "bags of water", would also be susceptible to the gravitational pull of the sun and the moon? Then the next logical step is that the other planets in the solar system may also influence us. Can this be true?

Astrologers will back up their point of view with graphs, charts and testimonials from people they have advised. The more scientific mind will scoff at the whole idea as utter nonsense. They will cite the laws of nature and physics to prove there is no scientific evidence – it is all hearsay.

So, is there something in it? Frankly, I don't know. (People see what they believe, not believe what they see.) The ancient astrologers did at least have a point. There are times when each of us has really exciting periods in our lives, all goes well, we can't seem to make a mistake, we are on a roll. There are times, equally, when we can't seem to get it together. Redoubling our efforts seems to drive us further from our goal. Nothing is going right and every step we take just makes matters worse – not better. Then there are other times when we are making some gains, some losses and, with any luck, actually making progress. The astrologers saw this and assumed it was caused by a relationship between your date, time and place of birth and the alignment of the planets.

Now look at the logical viewpoint. There are high and low points in everyone's life. There are times when you will do well financially, be on form and feel on top of the world. This is just the law of averages. Conversely, you will have low points, have no money and feel rejected. Again the law of averages. The rest of the time you will be at points in between, a kind of neutrality – getting by.

Getting By Or Going Up?

This is what life is for most people – getting by. Just enough money to pay the bills, feeling you are getting nowhere, making no progress. Getting demands from your boss, your spouse, your family, your friends. Feeling you don't have enough time. Feeling like a tennis ball, going forward and backward at the whims of others, having no real control over the outcome of the game. And for most people, it may as well be the law of averages, or the alignment of the planets. But is this the case for everyone? Are there exceptions? Is this for you? Welcome to the game of life!

The tennis ball is happiest going forward and back. That is the whole point of its existence. It can only be happy, only be fulfilled when it is being used with a tennis racquet and player – that is its sole function. It patiently waits its turn on a shelf, in a box or in somebody's pocket. It comes to life in the game. It is now in its flow. It is fulfilling its purpose. Aren't you excited for the tennis ball?

Now you are not a tennis ball – you are an intelligent being with incredible potential. But like the tennis ball, don't you want to get in your flow? Don't you want to fulfil your potential, have happiness and prosperity in your life? Wouldn't you like to awaken in the morning feeling excited because of the fun you are having in your life? Do you think this is farfetched? Well, consider this. Have you ever noticed how some people always land on their feet? They are on a roll. They attract money, success and fame. Apparently effortlessly.

It is as if they are standing on an escalator going up. Other than taking the steps onto the escalator, they just stand there and, like cream, rise to the top.

The rest of us are endeavouring to go up on an escalator that is going down. We have to climb the steps just to stand still. If we stop for even a few moments we have gone backwards and have to climb twice as fast just to get to the same spot. Bills and taxes have to be paid, so we put more effort in, climbing faster and faster and we seem to make no progress at all. Most are lucky just to stay in the same place. The people on the up escalator are in flow.

Consider the humble drinking straw. Hold it in the direction of the wind and it flows through, simply and easily. Hold it against the flow and the wind will bend it in half. A sailing ship travelling with the wind will travel as fast as the wind, with a minimal effort from the crew. Going in any direction other than the flow of the wind requires constant care and correction from skilled navigators and sailors.

You can be like the tennis ball, entirely dependent on others to have any purpose of existence or you can get into your own flow, taking full responsibility for your own advancement and not depending on any individual or group. So how do you tune in to this flow?

The Basic Principle

There is a principle upon which all life, all growth is based. Every living thing exists because of it. Most humans are aware of it but ignore it. Enlightened people accept and live by it. Being such a simple concept it is easy to overlook and pass by. An understanding of this principle will take you to a higher plane of existence. Please do not pay lip service to it. You will be repaid many times over for the time you spend contemplating it. Grasping it and putting it to work for you will give you a new level of awareness and unshakable inner strength.

Before we look at this principle let us again look at the three steps to accomplishing anything successfully.

Firstly you must define your purpose or goal – what you want to achieve. Let us say you want a tree in your back garden – an apple tree, that each autumn will bear its fruit of juicy, succulent apples. Secondly you must adopt the right procedures. In this case you must plant the seed in fertile soil. Thirdly, your attitude or mindset. Your attitude here is that in time the tree will grow and bear fruit.

The principle is as simple as this:

Plant the seed and the universe will give you the tree.

That's it. Having planted the seed you must not interfere with the flow of the universe. To do so could damage or kill the process. Once the seed is planted you must let the universe take over. It will provide the rain, the sunshine, the nutrients and you will get the tree.

The type of seed you plant depends on what kind of

tree you want. What seeds do you plant in your life? Are your crops worth cultivating? Are you asking the right questions?

Thomas Edison had an idea, a seed, in his mind. Experiment after experiment proved unworkable. But he believed he would get his "tree". The answer was the combination of elements and principles, which would make the electric light bulb. He found that answer and from that original seed grew an industry that not only made Edison a very rich man but also lit up the whole world.

Planting the right seeds is similar to asking the right questions. One man might ask how he can earn $1, another how to earn $100. Both bills are printed on the same paper using the same amount of ink. The manufacture of each requires the same amount of effort yet one is worth a hundred times more.

In learning to use your intuition you must learn to plant the right seeds by asking the right questions and then you must trust the universe to give you the right answers.

The Blocked Hose

You are going to water the garden. Off to the shed to find the garden hose. Unroll it, attach one end to the tap and turn on the water. What happens? Yes, the water should flow through the hose and out of the end. However, today, nothing is happening. You are surprised. Check the tap. Yes, it's working. But no water is coming out of the hose. Hmmm. Ah – perhaps you are standing on the hose? No, still no water. Let's check the hose itself. Ah – there is a kink near the tap end. Okay, straighten it out making sure the hose's memory doesn't put it back. Some water is coming out, but it is little more than a trickle. Check the hose again. There are two small leaks, a bend and a twist. Patch up the leaks and fully straighten out the hose. Now the water is flowing freely right through. Let's adjust the nozzle of the hose. By twisting the nozzle we are "tuning the flow". The water can now be directed and the force regulated. It can come out like a fast jet or a fine spray. Yet it is the same water flowing through the hose.

Just as the water flows through the hose, so does the natural flow of the universe flow through us. And, just as we can tweak the nozzle and get different results, so we can tweak the flow coming through us – using it for better results in our lives.

So how are you going to get the flow working in your life? Wherever you are in the world today reading this, you are surrounded by music. Maybe you can hear it and maybe you can't. If you can't and doubt me, just turn on a radio and tune it in. The music was there all the time. Re-tune the radio to a different station and you will hear different music. Please understand that the music is always there on various frequencies. You just have to put the radio in the flow of the music – tune it in.

Likewise, you need to just tune yourself into the frequency you want in your life. The flow is already there. All you need is to tune into it. But you must also make sure that you, the conduit, are not blocked. Firstly you put yourself in the flow by doing what you are supposed to do. Finding your purpose in life, what you should be doing and placing yourself in the marketplace. If you haven't already done so, go back to the chapter on working out your life's path.

A general in battle will look for his enemy's weakest point and concentrate all his might right there. He does not say, "Okay – I'll put a few men here and let the rest attempt some other areas and hope something will give way." No, he goes for the power of massive action, directed at the point of least resistance. In the original film *Star Wars* the good guys have found the weakness of the Death Star. One bomb, planted in exactly the right spot, will allow for the destruction of the entire Death Star. It is Luke Skywalker trusting the force within him who achieves the goal. He concentrated all his effort on this one task.

So in life. Do what you are most effective at doing and concentrate on that. Be the king of the hill in your field. Right, you know your purpose; you are out in the marketplace and ready for the forces of the universe to flow through you.

You Are Now One-Third of the Way There

The next step is to sharply focus on the results you want. Decide exactly and precisely the end result. Picture it in your mind. It might be a major promotion, a huge increase in earnings, a trip, a new car or all of these things. But for the sake of simplicity, let us imagine it is a doubling of your earnings. See that result in your mind. See it as though it already exists.

At the opening of the Epcot Centre near Disneyworld in Florida, a journalist said to Roy Disney, "It's a pity Walt wasn't here to see it." Roy, Walt's brother, replied, "Walt was the first to see it. That's why you can see it today." So write down the result you want on a card and carry it with you all the time. Read the card every morning when you get up and every night before you go to bed. Read it as many times as you can during the day. Each time, visualise yourself as having achieved this goal. The goal must be written in the present tense. "I earn £50,000 a year" or "I allow myself to earn £50,000 a year", not "I will earn ..." or "I hope to earn ..."

In your mental picture, see yourself as having achieved that goal. Act as you would expect to act with that salary.

The Secret to Understanding the Subconscious

Now your subconscious mind does not see you straight away as a £50,000-a-year earner, just as a £25,000 earner, so you will feel uncomfortable at the start. You will have negative thoughts, you will doubt that it can happen, and these thoughts will turn to fear and anxiety. It would be easier to give up your goal and stay the way you are. The main difference between a £25,000-a-year earner and a £50,000 earner is that the £25,000-a- year earner doesn't have the knowledge to become a £50,000-a-year earner or does have the knowledge but is too lazy to try.

As with everyone who starts something new, there are difficulties and setbacks. The baby who starts to learn to walk, falls many, many times before he learns just to stand up. Over a period of months he learns to stand, and then to walk and run. It would be daft for him to say after the first attempt, "This is too difficult. Why bother since crawling gets me around. I will stick with crawling." The same with learning to drive. There are many things to do, all seemingly at the same time and it is very confusing. But slowly, bit-by-bit, confusion leads to competency, which gives way to mastery. Driving the car becomes so embedded in your subconscious that you can do it very skilfully without thinking.

Once you understand that it will take your subconscious a while to accept these new instructions, all you need to do is consciously programme it by visualising and reading your goal. After a while, by force of habit, the old programming which sees you as a £25,000-a-year person, will be replaced by the new. Money is made mentally before it is collected physically. In your mind, you will be aware that there are a few differences between those who earn £25,000 and those who earn £50,000. Make a note in your mind of these differences or write them and begin to act them out in your daily life. Get going on the little things that £50,000-a-year earners do. Set out to act like a £50,000-a-year earner. Remember what Cary Grant said, "I have acted like Cary Grant for so long, I became him."

Bleach Your Mind

Also instruct your subconscious to let go of the old picture of you. Ever clean a filthy drain? There is a lot of gunge and goo clinging to the edges and usually a foul stench.

Out with the strong bleach. Squirt liberal doses into the drain and all around the edges. Instantly the dirt and grime begins to seep away. Streaks of cleanliness appear in front of your very eyes, like magic. Another squirt of bleach and the transformation is literally stunning. The stench is gone and the filth is no more.

Equally, your subconscious may already be conditioned with equally vile programming. If you are wounded physically you must patch yourself up and get on with it. If someone damaged your car, you would not spend the rest of your life complaining that your car had been damaged and you couldn't drive. It would be nothing more than a temporary inconvenience. You would have it patched up, repaired, mended and continue to drive it. Therefore do not spend the rest of your life complaining about something that happened in the past. Let go of it. If your mind is not working properly because of bad programming and conditioning we have to clean it.

Visualise the cells of your brain, caked with these old invalid pictures of yourself. Give them a liberal dose of bleach and see in your mind's eye the stinkin' thinkin' drip away, the grime and slime seep out, leaving those brain cells clean and refreshed, ready for new and positive pictures to replace them. It may take a number of cleansings to clear your old conditioning. Just like it will take a while for your hair to find a new way to grow when you change your hairstyle. So clear out the old and replace it with a picture of the results you want.

Paradoxically you may be blocking your own path to success. A poor man on a park bench sees another man driven in a limousine and he says to himself, "There but for me, go I." In other words, he is looking at the living embodiment of his own rejected thoughts. Both men would over the years have had similar thoughts and opportunities. One seized the day and went with them, sometimes meeting setback and failure, but slowly bit by bit achieving success. The other chose not to think the right thoughts and chose to let the opportunities slip by, risking nothing and achieving nothing.

Do you doubt that positive expectant visualisation can help you? Many people say well, it sounds good, but they don't try it, or they give up fairly quickly. If I could demonstrate to you that it undoubtedly works, wouldn't that make you want to give it your enthusiastic commitment?

WARNING!!!

Under NO Circumstances Attempt This Exercise

Read this but **DO NOT** try the exercise. Just imagine doing it.

Find somewhere quiet to sit where you won't be disturbed. No bright lights, phones switched off, no stereo or TV. No screaming children. Just calm, peace and quiet. Relax in your favourite armchair. Close your eyes. Take a few deep breaths. With each breath, your body feels more and more relaxed. Visualise yourself having a meal, cutting up the food, chewing it, swallowing it and digesting it further in your stomach. See it passing into your small intestine, which is like a long tube zigzagged, layer upon layer, one on top of the other. The food now passes into your large intestine, which goes like a loop from the lower part of your body up one side across and down to your colon, from where waste matter is passed out of the body.

Now start to imagine disease spreading from your colon up into your digestive system. Imagine yourself feeling ill, your digestive system failing to work and deteriorating with the spread of this disease. Visualise rot and decay spreading to your internal organs. See your insides putrefying and smelling like a bag of old forgotten rotting vegetables.

Imagine doing this exercise faithfully every day for thirty days. How do you think you would feel? I bet you are shuddering and cringing at the thought. You are probably saying, "No way – I'd be mad to do that!"

Under no circumstances should you try this exercise. Absolutely not at all. But the thought alone makes most people squirm. They believe that such a concept repeated regularly would invite, encourage and manifest disease. If you accept that thinking such negative thoughts would put you in a negative flow; if you accept that being tuned into sickness would attract disease into your life, then as night follows day tuning into positive healthy and happy thoughts must attract positive, healthy and happy things into your life. It is the law of cause and effect. The law of sowing and reaping. Again I repeat: **DO NOT try the above exercise**.

Springclean Your Life

Remember how we had to doctor the garden hose to let the water flow? For a moment, pretend the hose is a sentient being. It knows its purpose is for the flow of water. It can imagine and visualise itself watering the garden, in such a way that it sees rich, luscious grass and colourful blooming flowers. But unless the kinks, bends and twists in the hose are straightened out and the leaks mended, the hose cannot function efficiently or effectively. Once the blockages are removed, the hose goes from minimum flow to maximum flow in a few short seconds.

You are exactly the same. The kinks, leaks and blockages in the hose manifest themselves in your life as clutter. The very best thing you can do is get rid of the clutter in your life, yes, all the clutter. Everything.

Clear out your wardrobe. Get rid of the clothes you have not worn for over eighteen months. Especially that outfit that cost a lot of money and you wore only a few times. All those suits, jackets, sweaters, pullovers, old underwear and well-worn socks. Shoes that you haven't worn. Get rid of them all. If you must, have a garage or car boot sale or, better still, give them away – to someone, or some organization, that will benefit from them. It is highly unlikely that you will receive any direct benefit from this, but you will sooner or later receive an indirect benefit – usually in far greater proportion than you would have thought. Just cast your bread on the waters, give of yourself to the universe and do not expect anything in return.

Give to the Universe

This idea of giving without expecting something in return is alien to most people. Some are completely unable to give at all. Some years ago our family, through me, got to know a travelling entertainer whose work took him to Dublin during the winter months. Each Christmas Day we would invite him to our home for the afternoon and evening. As it is the custom to give gifts, however small, to friends and family on Christmas Day, we were surprised to see he always turned up empty-handed. Now, I wasn't expecting anything for myself but I felt it would be nice if he gave my mother something – even a small box of chocolates.

The third year, I bought and gift wrapped such a box and asked him to hand it to her. "I can't," he replied. "Well", I said, "don't say it's from you, just hand it to her." "You don't understand," he said. "I can't give, it's just not my nature."

It's like the story of the middle-aged man who fell into the river. A student standing at the bank reached out. "Give me your hand." The drowning man was within reach – no hand. Stretching his hand out as far as he could, the young man again said, "Give me your hand." No response.

Thinking quickly, he shouted, "Take my hand." The drowning man did so and was pulled out. He could not "give" his hand to save his life, but he could "take" the hand of another person to do so. Believe me, you do not want such thinking in your own life. It builds unhappiness, self-doubt and inner anxiety. You trust nobody and therefore nobody trusts you.

This does not mean that you should give away your skills and talents. You have a living to make and are on the way to a life of wealth and abundance. You must charge for your services and time. If they show up, bill 'em. If you are really good at what you do, your price will not be the main concern of your customer. If you need brain surgery do you look for the cheapest price or the best available surgeon? About ten per cent of your time and effort should go towards giving back without any expectation of reward.

A university professor, in search of enlightenment, visits a Zen Master and wants to learn his philosophy of life. The Master offers the professor a cup of tea, which he gladly accepts. In pouring the tea from the pot into the cup, the Master fills the cup to overflowing. The tea is spilling down the sides, filling the saucer and pouring onto the floor. The professor is stunned, embarrassed and confused. "Stop," he says. "The cup is already full." "And so is your head," says the Zen Master. "You must empty it before you can accept new ideas."

As the professor must let go of his earlier conditioning, so too must you let go of your clutter. Not just your clothes, but anything you no longer use. Old furniture you do not like, old magazines or books you know you will not refer to again.

You must also tend to unfinished business. You need to settle unpaid bills, tax matters that need sorting out, borrowed items that need returning to their owners.

The Artist Who Almost Was

In his book *The Experience of Magic*, Eugene Burger tells the story of visiting a friend, an artist, whose studio is full of paintings, but none are finished. All were enthusiastically started, and then halfway through, the artist went on to begin another canvas. The potential for power and greatness in his work is easily recognised. As none of his paintings are finished, can he be called an artist, or is he just a dabbler?

The story is a great lesson. Obviously, this man could be a great artist but the clutter of unfinished paintings in his life is his biggest obstacle. Finishing one and bringing it to the marketplace (selling it) could open doors that would lead to fame, prosperity and success. Finishing the paintings would create a flow, which would start off slowly but very quickly take off and soar to unimagined heights. Eugene's story had a profound effect on me, as I recognised my own unfinished projects.

By removing something you are creating a vacuum. Nature abhors a vacuum. So something must replace what has gone. By eliminating clutter, you are creating the circumstances for flow to come into your life, or you to come into the flow. If you have programmed yourself for the flow you want, that is what you will get.

This also works for governments. In 1997, Charlie McCreevey, the Irish Minister for Finance, reduced the Capital Gains Tax from forty to twenty per cent. The first year the lower rate was in place, the Government collected seven times more in Capital Gains Tax than they had ever taken in when the rate was forty per cent, so obviously there was a blockage there which, when released, brought money into the pockets of people who had things to sell and also into the Government's coffers.

Go for Self-Interest

Get rid of unresolved conflict. Forgiveness is important for eliminating clutter and guilt, which is heinous for holding people back. The four steps are:

1. Forgive those who have wronged you. Forgive them and forget them.
2. Forgive your parents for any real or imagined things they have done against you. Let it go – it's gone, it's in the past.
3. Make up and apologise to those you yourself have wronged.

4. Forgive yourself anything you have done in the past that is bothering you, that is making you feel guilty – let it go and forgive yourself.

You are doing this purely for self-interest. You are not forgiving others for their benefit, but for yours. By doing so you are freeing your self from the negative emotional ties that eat into your psyche.

Many of us hold grudges against our parents for endless different reasons. You might have done the same thing if the situation was reversed, or maybe they were completely wrong and caused you major hurt. Let go of the grudges. It is causing you not just clutter but a major blockage. Living in the past leads to insecurity, fear and depression.

Apologise to those you have wronged. Again, you are doing this for your benefit, not theirs. It will not be easy to do but it will unblock your inner being on a spiritual level.

Forgive yourself. Get rid of guilt. Refuse to tolerate it for even a moment. All the things you should have done, the things you did that you regret. Let them go. Just as clearing a blocked drain will allow the floodwater to disappear, forgiving yourself will cleanse your soul, and free your spirit to soar into the plane of higher things.

Another obstacle to flow is the fear of being resented. If, in the past, you resented people who had money, your inner being will battle against you having wealth, because you fear by having wealth, you too will be resented.

Perhaps the greatest obstacle of all to advancement in your life, the achievement of success and accumulation of wealth, is your friends and family. Yes, the people who you think would want, and probably do want, the best for you. But by achieving things you upset the status quo. Your peers are happy with their comfort zone. If you start to achieve more than the group expects, you are rocking the boat. The others start to feel uncomfortable. You are getting too big for your boots as far as they are concerned.

Intellectually and rationally, they will wish you well but subconsciously they will pull you back. Not only are you challenging their comfort zone but also your success is reflecting back to them their own lack of it. They do not want a constant reminder of their failure to do what they know they should be doing. They will systematically and subtly (sometimes not so subtly) pull you back to their level.

So if you embark on your life's adventure – key words – *your life's adventure* – not someone else's, you may have to shed some friends as well as the clutter. But shedding those who obviously aren't real friends, you will attract more successful people into your life. Remember, nature abhors a vacuum. Who do rich and successful people hang out with? Yes, other rich and successful people. So who do you want to hang out with? The successful, or those who are going nowhere?

Buckets of Abundance

Three people go to the sea. One takes a thimble; one takes a bucket and the other a barrel. They fill up their containers with water but each and any one of them could have taken a barrel or something larger. The sea does not care. The person who chose to take the thimbleful of water thought small. The person with the bucket thought bigger and the person with the barrel thought about as big as he could think with what was available. But remember, the sea does not care. You can go and take as much water as you want.

Because it is in flow, the water will in turn evaporate, turn to rain and come back and replenish the sea. The whole cycle will repeat itself. It is in flow. You can tap into that flow as much as you want, or as little as you want. The flow does not care.

If you were to go into an old house that had been locked up for a few years, what's the first thing you would do? You would open the windows to get rid of the old smelly, stagnant air. You would let fresh energy flow through the house and within a few minutes you could feel the change – you could sense the energy level in the whole building being uplifted. You do a bit of shaking. You get rid of the dust. You do a bit of spring-cleaning and after a while what was an old dusty, musty premises will become cleaner, brighter, sharper and you can feel the flow of energy throughout the house. It's the same thing in your life.

Tuning Into Flow

1) Know your purpose in life.

2) Know what you have to do and what needs to be achieved.

3) Keep checking that you are heading in the right direction. Make whatever adjustments are necessary to stay on track. Stay tuned in to the right wavelength.

4) Don't attempt too much at the start. You want your skills to be challenged, not overwhelmed. A rock climber does not start on Mount Everest.

5) Stay focused on what you are doing. Be in the moment. Do not be distracted by what you could be doing later.

6) When you are focused, involved and immersed in the task at hand all other problems and distractions disappear.

7) When in flow you feel in control of your life. Feelings of self-consciousness disappear. You feel you are going beyond yourself.

8) In a state of flow time does not seem to exist. Hours pass by in minutes, yet a specific event that lasts only a few seconds may replay itself very slowly and you can accurately recall every last detail.

When in flow, you are in harmony with the universe. You are part of the symphony of all things. Avoid clutter and conflict which will silence your music and block your flow.

"I bargained with life for a penny
And life would pay no more;
However I begged at evening
When I counted my scanty store.

For life is a just employer:
He gives you what you ask,
But once you have set the wages,
Why you must bear the task.

I worked for a menial's hire
Only to learn dismayed,
That any wage I had asked of life,
Life would willingly have paid."

Napoleon Hill

***"Remove emotional scars with forgiveness."* Dr Maxwell Maltz**

CHAPTER 8

Amazing Coincidences

What is a coincidence? My dictionary defines it as "a remarkable concurrence of events or circumstances without apparent casual connection".

Let us be objective here. I come from a conjuring background. I know how easy it is to be deceived by normal and natural occurrences. What people see and what they perceive are two different things. Interestingly, the more educated you are, the easier it is to fool you. Fake psychics doing cleverly disguised magic tricks can easily mislead many scientists and researchers. When a professional magician has been called in, he has frequently detected trickery. It is a magician's job to fool people and he knows what to look for. So when unusual things have happened, I have naturally been sceptical.

Statisticians can predict that so many of the population will die before the age of ten, twenty, thirty and so on. They just don't know who. They are working on the law of averages. The odds against you winning the lottery are very high, say a million to one. The odds against you winning the lottery twice are millions and millions to one. However, somebody, somewhere, regularly wins the lottery. And the odds against somebody, somewhere, winning the lottery twice aren't really much greater than winning it once, but the odds against a *specific* person winning once are very high. The odds against that *specific* person winning twice are truly astronomical.

The stories that follow are remarkable. To me, they indicate something more than coincidence. They are all by people I know (or me) and all the stories are first hand. They are all by level-headed and basically sceptical people.

Coincidence or Providence?

Eric Sharp woke at 4am. His wife Muriel was in hospital and he felt something was wrong. He arrived at the hospital thirty minutes later, to find the ward sister at the telephone trying to contact him, as his wife was in much distress and wanted him to be with her.

The Last Flight leaves at 3pm

Back in 1942, whilst doing military service, Eric was stationed at the Takoradi RAF Base, on what was then known as the Gold Coast (Ghana) in North Africa. Eric worked in the Officers' Mess. One of the perks was being able to get a flight on one of the planes. Eric had never flown before and had his name down. It was something he was really looking forward to.

Serving breakfast one morning, he approached the test flight CO and asked if there was anything available that day. "There is a plane going up at three this afternoon. You can have a flight in the gun turret of that, and your friend Milli, who has flown before can come along too, as there may be another place." Eric was excited, and he and his friend left the camp at 1pm, as it was nearly a two-hour walk around the swamp to the aerodrome. Now, if Eric makes an appointment, he always keeps it. Never does he change his mind. However, they were only a few steps on the way when Eric said, "Milli, it's a hot day, let's go swimming instead."

Returning from the swim at 3.30pm, they noticed an aircraft overhead in difficulties, with smoke pouring from it. It eventually crashed upside down in the swamp, killing everyone on board, including the person who took Eric's place.

Eric had never met the other man, who took his place on that flight. It turned out that he had the same rank as Eric; his surname was also Sharp, with the same spelling. His serial number was **12105**49. Eric's was **12105**27, only the last two digits differing.

The Tumbling Block

In the early 1970s, Eric and his friend Reg Simpson attended an auction at the Magic Circle headquarters in Chennies Mews, London. The auditorium was under a dome of glass, decorated with signs of the zodiac. Eric and Reg took their seats at 3pm. Eric could see the item he wanted would not come up until 6pm. He decided to stay, as he particularly wanted it. Suddenly for no reason, just before 3.30 he said to Reg, "Let's go," and they left.

Much later that night, Eric got a call from another magician. "Eric, remember you and your friend left today? Two others took your seats. Just a couple of minutes later, two blocks came crashing through the glass roof and landed on them. They are in hospital."

Eric does not know why he left, and is also aware that it was 3.30 when the bricks came down through the roof, the same time the aircraft had crashed thirty years previously.

Generation To Generation

In the 1950s, Eric was a member of a number of magical societies. He would have read of magicians visiting or retiring to South Wales. He had never been in touch with any of them. In 1956, he read that Rex Daina had retired to the area. Eric had never heard of him and knew nothing about him. For some reason Eric had the urge to call on him. It turned out Rex had had a severe stroke, which forced his retirement as a society entertainer in London. He and Eric got on well together and Eric would take him up to London on trips whenever he was going.

One day, out of the blue, he offered to teach Eric Punch and Judy. He was an excellent tutor. The puppet show increased Eric's bookings by ninety per cent.

In 1973, aged seventeen, I wrote to Eric. Having made up a trick he had described in a magazine I just wanted to thank him for publishing it. That's all. It so happened the week my letter arrived, Eric had broken his leg, and had some time off from his busy schedule. He replied and after a couple of letters, out of the blue, he offered to teach me Punch and Judy. Meeting Eric was the best thing that ever happened to me in my career as an entertainer.

A Mother's Bond

Richard Busch from Pittsburgh contributed this story and here it is in his own words: *"As a well-known skeptic, I rather doubt the claims of so-called 'psychic' powers such as ESP and telepathy. However, as a spontaneous, uncontrollable event possibly requiring unknown specific conditions, perhaps human intuition can offer us all at least a fascinating invitation to sensitively pay better attention to ourselves and the world around us. Most people are chronically too hurried and mindlessly numb to really notice and pay quality attention to much of anything. But what follows is a true story of human intuition and sensitivity. Or perhaps, it suggests that sincere love and caring knows no bounds! This you must decide for yourself. In any case, what follows is absolutely true.*

"While back in college in 1971, I used to call my mother every Sunday, on the long distance. It was cheaper than calling on a weekday and money was especially tight in those days. On a very unforgettable Monday and one day after the weekly call, I was studying at my desk in the dorm room when the strangest feeling came over me. My hand shot out, picked up a dime (this was 1971!!) and I found myself walking to the pay phone in the hall. I put the coin in and heard myself announce to the long-distance operator that I wished to make a long-distance call to [my mother's name] and I gave the number. It was so strange. I had nothing special to say and yet the call was being made. Why? For what purpose? What exactly was I spending good money on when I had just made a call the previous day at a lower phone rate? I honestly had no idea!!

"It was as if something was making me call against my will. I even tried to hang up the receiver but my hand wouldn't or couldn't do it. I honestly was confused and puzzled at my own inexplicable actions!! Why was I doing this???

"As soon as the receiver was picked up on the other end and my Mother said 'hello,' I started frantically apologizing immediately: 'Mom, please forgive me, but I have absolutely no idea why I am calling!' ... Silence ... She then slowly replied, "but I know exactly why you called!"

"We were very, very close, always, and could communicate with each other on special, even secret non-verbal levels. And you should understand that my mother was dying of a terminal disease. I knew that. Then she told me that she had JUST THAT MINUTE received a call that her Uncle had passed away ... and then seconds later the phone rang

again and ... it was me. Her Uncle was indeed buried a few days later. And a few months after that, my Mother was laid to rest just a few feet away from him. She knew this was her destiny!

"What surely must have been surging through my Mother's mind? What emotions, worry, concern, and in my Mother's case, unselfish love, a very rare and special love that always reached out to others?

"I think 'SOMETHING' was 'intuitively' received by me from my Mother in that very unique, once-in-a-lifetime moment of intense emotional surge concerning life and death from an unimaginable emotional depth from the deepest of human pathos. AND I AM A SKEPTIC! But I have no other adequate explanation, except that I, to this day, will set no limits, boundaries, or barriers to my Mother's love and what her feelings surely must have been at that moment! Our special connection somehow bridged time and distance at that very instant. And is it not one of our purposes on Earth to yearn to bridge that gap, that unknowable abyss from here ... to there, to always learn more and expand the human condition?

"Far from being 'psychic' which I per se reject, perhaps this is what it really means to accept an expanded appreciation of our humanness?"

An Unexpected Visitor

In April 1998, the Society of Irish Magicians was having its annual dinner. As President, I was host to our visiting entertainer, Trevor Lewis from North Wales. That night, as my houseguest, Trevor was in the front guest bedroom, and I was in the rear bedroom. Normally, in the house, I lock all the windows but leave the small bathroom window slightly ajar. At night I would usually lock the bathroom door from the outside. Even though I felt the window was too small for any intruder to enter there was no point in taking chances. The locked door would stop them.

As Trevor was an overnight guest, I did not lock the

bathroom door. He might need to use it during the night and it is awkward fiddling for keys and light switches in an unfamiliar house.

At five in the morning my bedroom door handle turned, awakening me. "Hello," I called, thinking it was Trevor forgetting which room he was in. I heard footsteps, and then the burglar alarm went off. "What is he up to?" I thought. "Sleepwalking perhaps."

I got up and went down the stairs, turned off the alarm and closed the front door, which was wide open. I found the bathroom window also wide open. A burglar! Further investigation revealed the intruder's jacket and sweater in the garden, which he had removed before climbing up the pipes and in through the window. Open windows do not affect the alarm in my house, only heavy vibrations.

The police arrived within minutes. There were fingerprints and muddy footprints everywhere, as well as the garments. Interestingly, with all the clues and evidence, the police never caught the intruder. The coincidence here is that the one day I have a guest, the day I do not lock the bathroom door, is the day I have a burglar.

Let me add here that I had figured sooner or later by the law of averages I would probably be burgled and had made up my mind in advance that I would not let it affect me. One of those things that happen. You hear of people who feel they have been violated, their inner sanctum destroyed or desecrated, and they would never live in that house again. That, I had decided in advance, was not the path for me, but there is more to the story.

The following day Trevor left on the ferry. That night I made sure that all the windows and doors were locked, especially the bathroom window and door. I double-checked everything. I locked my bedroom door from the inside.

Getting into bed, I found it difficult to slep. The late night of the dinner the evening before, plus the early awakening by the burglar, meant I was overtired. I tossed and turned in the bed and suddenly the burglar alarm went off. I was out of my bed in a flash. "He's back," I thought. I rushed downstairs to the alarm, switching it off. I phoned the police urging them to come quickly as the intruder was back. Obviously, I thought, to collect his clothes. I checked all the doors and windows. No sign of a break-in.

One of the scams in a burglar's bag of tricks is to set off your alarm. You check everything and re-set the alarm. He sets it off again. After this happens a few times, you think there is a fault with the system and leave it off. That is when he breaks in. Perhaps, I thought, this is what he is up to! I turned off all the lights and lurked in the kitchen looking to see if he would return. Nothing. I meandered through the dimness into the front room. Looked out. Nothing. In the shadows, I felt like an intruder in my own home. After thirty minutes of checking the front and the rear of the house there was no sign of the burglar or the police. I decided to go back to bed.

The alarm would not re-set. "Zone A", it kept flashing. I didn't know which was Zone A. The alarm had been installed ten years previously and I had to go looking for the instructions. Zone A is the personal attack button, of which there are two. One beside the front door and the other beside my bed. In twisting and turning, the duvet had hit against the button. It had never done that in ten years, and now the night after I do have a burglar, it goes off.

Overnight Delivery: Federal Express's Turning Point

Gardner Symonds, who built Tenneco into a million-dollar company, said there were four things needed to build a successful business:

1. Find the capital.

2. Deploy it in a favourable environment.

3. Employ the right people.

4. You have got to know when to get the hell out of the way. That's the hardest part, but that's the one that will make you rich.

Here's a story to illustrate that fourth point – and it has a happy coincidence!

The Federal Express (now called FedEx) start-up date was March 12th, 1973. Mike Basch was vice-president for sales and customer service. In spite of all his efforts, fewer than ten packages per night were shipped the first week. There were only four weeks left of cash flow or the company would go under.

Extra sales teams were sent to more cities, including a town in Indiana. RCA were there, and shipped twenty packages a day. After camping outside his office, the top Federal Express salesman got to see the chief executive of RCA. He was turned down. He offered free delivery for a week. No!

Two weeks later, the situation still bleak, at three-thirty in the afternoon, Diane, a secretary, was holding forth at the head office. The mission of the company was "Get the packages delivered – no matter what."

Mike Basch says, "Given the opportunity, people left to their own devices, with an idea in mind will do what is necessary to build the business. Too often managers get in the way with rules and procedures."

Here is what happened. Diane gets a call from a distraught lady in Indiana. "I am getting married tomorrow, and my wedding dress has not arrived. I am from a small town and mine is the only wedding here this year, so it is a big event, not just for me, but for the whole community."

Diane tracks the package to Detroit, Michigan, three hundred miles away. She books a Cessna plane and a pilot to collect and deliver the package. It gets there that night. Monday morning Diane gets a call from the lady who asks to speak to a manager. She gets put through to Mike Basch. "I want to thank you for saving my wedding," she said. "My dress arrived on time but there is some bad news. I am from a small community and everyone at the wedding was talking about this amazing company that flew in my dress. I wasn't the centre of attention after all."

Mike asked Diane, "What prompted you to spend $300 dollars in shipping that dress?" "Well, you said the mission of the company was to get the packages delivered no matter what." "Yes, but to spend $300?" "Well, I figured we were going bankrupt anyway so what's the difference?"

Here's the coincidence: Some RCA executives were at the wedding and told their boss of this amazing company with such incredible service. The follow-up of the story was that Federal Express got the business from RCA.

The Car Door

When I was about seven years old, I was going for a drive one afternoon with my father in his car. For some strange reason, instead of sitting in the front passenger seat, I decided to sit in the rear seat. So, in I climbed and we were driving along the road when the front passenger door opened suddenly as we were turning a corner. Had I been sitting there I would have been thrown out and seriously injured or possibly killed. What made me decide to sit in the rear seat? I don't know. I normally would have been there because I was quite excited as any small child would be to be sitting up front, but for this particular day I sat in the back. We found afterwards there was a fault in the door and even though it looked closed, the lock on it was not working and any sudden pressure could have just swung it wide open.

The Parable of the Refuse Sack

Everyone said I should do something about my back garden. It wasn't large, but it was overgrown with weeds. So I had it dug out. It yielded five large refuse sacks of garden waste, and were they heavy! I put them out the front with another black bag of household waste. The refuse truck would call the following morning.

In Ireland, the garbage men are not obliged to take garden waste. But everything was concealed inside the sealed bags so I figured they wouldn't realise what was in there. I had read that a local council in England sued a householder for having extra heavy refuse sacks. One of the collectors had damaged his back in lifting it. So I took five sheets of A4 paper and with a thick marker labelled them "HEAVY". These I put in five clear cellophane bags and taped them to the refuse sacks. Thus, the signs were waterproof and, as they were taped down, couldn't blow away.

Next morning I left early for a business meeting, checked the bags were okay, and off I went. Returning at 11am the bags were still sitting patiently outside my home. Everyone else's refuse had been taken. Not mine! I couldn't believe it. I was furious. Why, those so and so's! I have been living here for years. I give them a bonus at Christmas. I hardly ever leave out more than one bag. Now that I need them, they desert me. The cheek of them! What should I do?

I loaded the five heavy bags into the back of my van and drove down the road where the head office of the refuse service was located. I stopped and unloaded the sacks right outside their gate. I hoped someone would come out. I would tell them what I thought of them. How dare they not take my bags. Me, a right thinking, tax-paying citizen. Was I full of righteous indignation! As it happened nobody came out. I just left the bags and drove away. Later that afternoon I was feeling a little tired and dozed off. Five minutes into it, I sat straight up.

The bin men come on Wednesday morning. This was Tuesday!

Boy, did I feel daft!! Later I explained it to the bin men who had a laugh and I gave them an extra bonus at Christmas.

There are some lessons to be learned here. Firstly and

obviously, get your facts right. Frequently you will have to make choices without being able to get all the facts. Fine. Just make sure the facts you do have are correct. Once, some years ago, I turned up at a function in a private house. I introduced myself. The lady was surprised. She explained the party was the following week. At least I wasn't a week late!

Secondly, don't be afraid to laugh at your own mistakes. Show a good sense of humour. Some people go to great lengths to cover up an error. They will be highly embarrassed to admit they ever made a mistake. Remember, we are all human. Don't be afraid to share your mistakes as well as your triumphs. You and others can learn from both. You will actually learn more from a mistake than a success. A good sense of humour is a sign of a healthy personality.

Thirdly, when we are in the wrong we tend to blame others. Now I knew the binmen did not have to take the garden waste. I became very indignant when they didn't. It was their fault as far as I was concerned, even though deep down I knew I was in the wrong. People who get pulled over for speeding are the same. Has that cop got nothing better to do? Here I am, a law-abiding citizen enjoying my car. Why isn't he out catching murderers and robbers? Hey, come on, he's doing his job. You are breaking the law. Maybe he is saving you from an accident.

Gut Instinct and Gut Reaction

Don't confuse gut instinct with gut reaction. Gut reaction is making a decision without studying all the facts you could have to hand. I went ahead and purchased the balloon machine in this story without doing any research, which I should have done. However, as you will see the story has an interesting twist as it led to something else.

In 1990 I was looking for another product to add to the range of services we offer party organisers and gift purchasers. I saw an ad for a 'teddy bear in a balloon' machine. This amazing device, shaped like a dustbin, inflated round balloons to sixteen inches (40cm) diameter in such a way that you could place a teddy inside them. Basically there was a suction motor in the base, similar to that found in a vacuum cleaner. The lid was airtight and the mouth of the large balloon was stretched open by a device built into the lid. When switched on, air was sucked into the balloon and the vacuum generated in the machine held it open. You could reach through the mouth of the balloon, which was stretched open to about five inches (13cm) in diameter and place in it tissue paper, a teddy bear, a bottle of champagne, or whatever would fit. I thought, "Wow, everyone will want one of these 'gifts in a balloon' to take home."

So I bought a machine and took space in a shopping centre during Easter week. Well, we hardly sold any. People thought the balloon would burst or deflate before they got it home. We had some entertainer balloons with us, the long skinny ones you twist into animals. We made up a few and they sold like hot cakes. "Wow! Hello! Is there a business opportunity here?" Yes, we did very well from the brightly coloured hats and animals we made. Had we not taken the space with the machine, we might never have found out. Now you regularly see clowns selling these balloon shapes at fairs and on the streets. We were the first to do it in Ireland. One door closes and another opens.

The Cheek Of Her

A young man was driving his open convertible up a mountain road. It was a lovely warm day and he was enjoying the sunshine, the breeze and the car. Suddenly another car, driven somewhat erratically by a woman, came around the bend. "Pig!" she shouted as she passed. Taken aback, he quickly recovered and roared, "Cow!" Feeling pleased at his quick retort he drove around the corner and hit the pig.

"You may depend on the inner mind absolutely. Everything you need to know will come to you when you need to know it."

"Man is blind until he achieves insight and he is deaf until he hears the inner voice of his own being."

"The hole you give through is the hole you receive through."

"No problem ever comes to you for which the answer is not already within you."

Dr Edward Kramer

CHAPTER 9

There's Method in the Madness

The snowflakes fell gently on New York City. Rush hour was over but the streets were busy enough with traffic. The constant honking of cars weaving their way across lanes was lost on the young couple who seemed caught up in the magic of the forthcoming festive season. Being early December, all the stores had been busy preparing their Christmas windows, vying to create the brightest, most colourful and attractive displays.

The pair, in their early twenties, were taking their time, going from window to window, almost like little children, absorbing the splendour, inventiveness and originality of the window dressing.

One window, yielding expensive gifts, gave way to an animated scene of the North Pole, with Santa and his elves busy preparing presents for all the good children. Another window showed the latest toys – the current crazes as advertised on TV, another showcased sparkling jewellery that would give Liberace a run for his money.

As they ambled silently along, holding hands, soaking in the visual feast, they came to a window that had just the crib in it. The infant Jesus, with Mary and Joseph, the shepherds, the cow and the donkey. "I don't believe it," uttered the man in astonishment, more to himself than his girlfriend, "now they are bringing religion into it."

Religion, Spirituality and Intuition

For the purpose of discussion we will look upon religion as belief systems structured by rules and regulations. Religion is the male, the yang side of the mirror, spirituality is the yin, female, receiving side.

While you study religion, you *go* to church, while your spiritual awareness *comes* to you. This chapter is where you discover how to get in touch with your spiritual, knowing, intuitive side, how to tap into infinite intelligence, the Christ force, the flow of the universe.

There are many ways your intuition comes to you, usually when you least expect it. It might be in a dream, having a conversation or playing golf. But the main way to **actively** tap into your intuition is through meditation. Don't be put off by this as it may bring to mind chanting hordes of religious zealots or images of individuals going into long self-induced hypnotic states. Meditation can be as simple as a few snatched minutes of relaxation or concentration. At least see it as time spent devoid of outside distractions and the internal chatter of ego. By actively tapping into intuitive intelligence I mean to deliberately put yourself in a state, such as relaxation, where your intuitive feelings can openly come to you.

Time to Relax

It can be difficult to take some time out to relax, meditate and get in touch with yourself, never mind finding the meaning of the universe. Rita Davenport from Phoenix, Arizona, is a busy professional speaker and TV host. A teacher of relaxation and meditation techniques approached her. He pointed out that her busy professional schedule, coupled with her family life, must cause a certain level of stress. He pointed out how beneficial the methods he could teach her would be. She agreed to give it a go. Consulting her diary, she reckoned the only time available was 7.45 in the morning. "But, I don't get up until 10am," was the astonished reply. No wonder the guy had such a relaxed lifestyle. If you fall into the latter category, you might want to skip this chapter. On the other hand, if you are always trying to meet deadlines, feel rushed, fitting as much as possible into your day, you will find the following ideas and techniques a godsend.

The first of three main ways of using your superconscious is to concentrate one hundred per cent on the problem, question or goal. Really work at it, like a dog with a bone, or a puppy with a blanket. Completely immerse yourself in it. Put the problem on paper, in as few words as you can. This alone will help prompt the solution.

The second way is to let go and do something completely different, like going to a movie, taking a walk, cleaning the house or simply meditate.

The third and optimal method is to combine the above two.

"The Mountain Comes to Mohammed"

The methods that follow will help you relax and allow the answers you are looking for to come to you. Even if you have no pressing need for answers, some of the approaches are excellent for re-vitalising the body and spirit. It may be a really busy day for you, you didn't sleep well the night before, you had a row with your spouse, a relation is ill, your boss is agitated, and work is piling up.

The best thing you can do is take time out. This is not a coffee break, a cigarette break, or a signal to chat with your colleagues about the latest TV soap drama. No. It is taking five minutes to tune yourself in, re-charge your batteries and clear your mind. This will give you the energy and focus to return to the task at hand in a fresher, calmer and unhurried state of mind, with the inner glow of confidence that you are in charge, and that things will get done.

If you regularly use the techniques, you will relieve stress and add years to your life. If you are on a long car journey and feel yourself falling asleep at the wheel, pull over, do the first method for five or ten minutes and feel wonderfully refreshed.

Relaxing!

Here are two excellent steps for getting into a relaxed state. You might like to read this section onto audiotape and play it back when you want to relax.

Sit comfortably with your back straight but not rigid. You should not be slumped. Legs spread apart and feet planted firmly on the floor. Arms can be crossed or uncrossed, with palms facing upward. Backs of hands should rest comfortably on your legs. Take a few deep breaths and close your eyes. Feel the air filling your lungs. Be aware of your breathing. On breathing in, say silently to yourself, "I breathe the universe." On breathing out, say, "The universe is breathing me." Do this for a few more breaths. You will feel your body relaxing.

Now concentrate on your left big toe. Feel it relaxing. You can do this in your mind's eye, or actually feel your big toe relaxing. Both work. If you find difficulty in visualising your toes and feet relaxing, just start off telling your big toe to relax and then tell your other toes, and continue telling each part of your body to relax as you proceed. Depending on your state you may see, hear or feel "the scene". Do what is best for you.

Feel all the stress draining away from your left big toe. Drifting and draining away. It is feeling totally, completely, entirely relaxed. All tension is erased; there is only contentment and calm in your big toe. Visualise this relaxation spreading to the other toes on your left foot. It may be a gentle slow spread, or perhaps your big toe can no longer contain its abundance of relaxation and it bursts, flowing into the adjoining toes. Feel the toes becoming fully relaxed. Now, that relaxation is spreading into your left foot, filling it entirely, spreading, creeping slowly to your ankle and up your leg, your calf muscles, your shin, your knee, up your thigh to the top of your leg. Your whole left leg is fully and completely relaxed. See it in your mind and feel it.

Now focus your attention on your right big toe and repeat the procedure, until both legs are fully relaxed. The first time you do this you will be distracted by other thoughts, your mind will be racing. That is totally natural and understandable. As with all skills, it will improve with practice. Even if it is not totally satisfactory the first time, you will see a big difference and it will get better and better each time you complete it. When you are distracted, just smile to yourself, because you understand what is happening and then return to the point you left off.

When your legs are fully relaxed, concentrate on your left thumb, seeing and feeling it becoming relaxed, the fingers, palm, wrist, forearm, elbow, upper arm, shoulder. Then the same with the right arm. Now feel the relaxation spreading from the top of your legs into your lower stomach, your inner organs, up through your ribcage, upper chest and shoulders.

Give a little extra time to your neck and shoulders as there is a lot of tension here. Feel the relaxation spreading up your neck, into your jaw, cheeks, past your ears, your eyes, right up to the top of your head and over your forehead. Feel your whole body, totally and completely relaxed. Take a few more deep breaths.

This is not a nap, you are conscious, and you are fully relaxed. You can stay this way for a while, continue with further steps or just come back to full awakening. If you choose to wake up now, just tell yourself you are fully refreshed, and open your eyes. Doing this for five to ten minutes will work wonders.

To continue with the second step: Count slowly from 1 to 20, feeling more relaxed and tranquil with each step, feeling completely at peace with yourself and the universe. Release all feelings and emotions, feel peace, love, inner wealth. You are in touch with your inner being. As you count up to 20, and as you reach 20, bask in the sheer glow of wonderfulness.

Stay in this state, as long as you like, and when you wish to return to the outer world, start counting backwards, until you reach 1, at which point you will open your eyes.

As you are counting backwards, instruct yourself on how you want to feel when you open your eyes. Think revitalised, full of energy, calm, inspired, ready for action – whatever feeling you want will be yours. Just concentrate on it as you count backwards, realising that when you get to 1, you will open your eyes, be fully awake and feeling terrific.

The Fireball Technique

Having reached a stage of complete relaxation, focus your attention on your navel area. Feel your entire power coming from that area. Imagine this power like a ball of fire. Right in your centre. Feel that ball of fire radiating intensely, like a miniature sun inside you. Feel its energy radiating down through your legs, into the earth. Feel it radiating up through your body, surging up through your head and into the heavens. Feel the power. Open your eyes, stand up and shake yourself out. Close your eyes and again feel that power within you. Take a few deep breaths; allow your mind and body to feel calm and relaxed.

You can now continue with your work and if you feel sidetracked at all, close your eyes for just a few moments and feel that power within you radiating throughout your whole body. You can do this last bit as often as you need to during the day, as it takes only a few seconds.

The Picture Technique

Let your body relax as in step one, and visualise a scene from nature that has great personal appeal for you. Perhaps you are surveying a magnificent view, you are on a mountain, in a field, beside a lake, or beside the sea. It may be somewhere that has strong memories for you or somewhere you would like to visit. If you are having difficulty visualising such a scene, choose a painting you particularly like and use that. It should be a scene from nature, quiet, calm and relaxing. See yourself in this scene, surrounded by and at one with the forces of nature.

Be aware of everything around you. Soak it all in. Picture all the colours, the different hues, appreciate the shapes of the trees, the plants, the animals, notice the clouds taking shape and moving, the water flowing. Hear all the sounds, no matter how small, and if any are indistinct focus in on them. As you breathe, smell the aromas, the fragrances. Breathe them in and savour them. Feel the movement around you, the breeze, the flight of the birds, the animals you can see and the ones you can't. Feel the movement in the earth beneath you. Feel the movement of the water and the life it contains. Drink the water, taste the fruit of the trees, the nectar from the flowers, be totally at peace with the scene you are a part of.

Breathe in and out, concentrating on its rhythm. In this state, allow your intuition to reveal itself to you. Do not go looking for answers; permit the answers to come to you. Whatever thoughts float through your mind, describe them aloud. If possible, use a tape recorder. Otherwise a friend with pen and paper would help. You can change places later and you can record your friend's thoughts. If you cannot record them as you speak, write them down immediately after you have finished.

Describe your feelings, what you see, hear, touch, taste and smell. Everything, no matter how trivial. Whatever thoughts and pictures come into your mind. Note it all. Later you will come to interpreting these thoughts. Do not fight the direction you are going. Allow yourself to be led. You will be amazed at what will be revealed to you. I promise. Later in this chapter I will show you how to interpret your intuitive thoughts and feelings.

The Animal Technique

You have met someone and are not sure how you feel about him or her. This technique is excellent for tapping your intuitive feelings about somebody. It can be used for both personal and business relationships.

Sit comfortably, relax, take a few deep breaths and picture the person you want to know more about. See them in your mind's eye. Allow the person to turn into an animal. What attributes does this animal suggest to you? A tiger might be menacing and attacking, or strong, gentle and protective. Is it young or old? Notice all its characteristics. Does any part of it become more prominent or particularly attract your attention? See the animal moving. Where is it going and what is it doing? What qualities suggest themselves to you? When you open your eyes, analyse what this means to you.

A tennis player tried this technique on herself. She thought she would see herself as a tiger on the court, strong and methodical, fierce and competitive. Instead, the animal that came to mind was the gazelle, swift and light-footed, which she realised was, in her case, more accurate.

You can also use this technique to answer a question. Close your eyes, take three deep breaths, repeating the question to yourself a few times and then allow the animal image to form. Continue as above, asking yourself the questions to interpret the answer.

Focus On An Object

Sit down, relax and take a few deep breaths. Ask yourself the question you want answered. Now the question must be as specific as possible. Questions such as "Why am I not rich?" "Who will I marry?" "Will I win the lottery?" "Will I get promoted?" are too general and susceptible to outside influences. They are not under your direct control. The more specific and precise the question, the clearer and speedier the answer. "What is the one thing more than anything else that is blocking money from flowing into my life?" "Who do I need to be to attract my ideal mate?" "What is blocking my career at the moment?" "What is the one thing I should be doing to attract the attention of my superiors that will rocket me upwards in my work and career?" These are the kind of questions you need to ask.

Now focus on some object in the room. Something that appeals to you. Maybe a flower, a picture, a clock. Focus on it and allow the image it forms in your mind to change. It may blur, go all fuzzy, change shape or transform into different images. Record or make mental notes of everything that comes to your mind, the objects, shapes, colours, smells, sensations and feelings.

The Borrowed Genius

In Chapter 5 we discussed the Imaginary Mastermind idea generation method. This version stems from that. Dr Win Wenger developed what he calls The Borrowed Genius Technique. Decide what genius from history you want to advise you and what your problem or question is. Sit back, relax and take a few deep breaths. Close your eyes and see yourself in a tranquil state, perhaps in a beautiful garden or in a scene from a painting. Describe aloud what you see. Explore the scene. Now your visitor arrives to see you. Describe him (or her) in full detail, his appearance, mannerisms, clothing etc. Imagine now lifting off his head and lowering it over your own like a helmet or mask. Make sure the eyes, ears, mouth and nose are fully aligned with yours.

You are now looking out through his eyes. Describe out loud what he sees. It may be the same scene or a different one. Let the images flow. Now turn your thoughts to the question. Let your "Borrowed Genius" look it over. Again describe out loud what he sees.

There was a point in his life when his genius was at its peak. Allow yourself to feel this. Feel how he felt. Describe it aloud. You are now nearly ready to come back to yourself. Visualise a full-length mirror in front of you and you see his reflection in it. Allow the mirror to fade away.

He is now standing in front of you. He has his own head back. You are again two separate beings. Ask him your question. What does he want to tell you? You will be surprised by his advice! Write down all your insights from this exercise.

Solitude

Excellent and practical as the above methods are, there is nothing like solitude for getting in touch with your inner self. A walk up the mountains, through the woods or along the beach on your own. At home close the doors, switch off the phones and any other external interruptions. You may choose to do nothing or just to contemplate. The main thing is you have time on your own. Performing one of the above intuitive exercises after a period of solitude will prove extremely beneficial.

The Yoga Lady

Yoga teacher Karen Ward told me this story about one of her pupils, a married woman with five young children. She had been on anxiety relieving drug Valium, since the birth of her first child. Turning up at the doctor's surgery for a renewal of her prescription, she was surprised to find the practice now being run by his son. He talked over her problems and handed her a note. Imagine her surprise at the pharmacy when they handed back her prescription saying they couldn't fill it. It read, "Do yoga."

Yoga was a subject she knew nothing about and her enquiries led her to Karen's class. Although completely sceptical she decided to give it a go. During one of the exercises she actually fell asleep. Karen gave the class an assignment. Find just five minutes each day for yoga breathing.

Returning home to her family she explained she would have homework to do each day, a notion her children found hilarious. The following evening her husband called the children together: "Mammy is going to do her homework upstairs. We will stay down here and there will be no noise and no interruptions."

Upstairs in her bedroom was the first time since the birth of her first child she knew she would have uninterrupted time to herself. She did her five minutes of relaxation. It felt great. No noise from downstairs. She took another five minutes. She relaxed for a further twenty minutes before descending. She felt terrific.

The following evening her husband again gathered the children: "Mammy needs her half-hour for her homework. Remember, no noise." (Notice how the five minutes had grown to thirty without her asking). Each day she now used that valuable time of solitude to do her five minutes of breathing and then pamper herself in some way, like doing her nails or having a relaxing bath.

Finding herself tuning into her body and what it wanted, it became easy to come off the Valium. If a mother of five young children can find a few minutes a day to meditate, anyone can.

Using Music

"Music hath charms to soothe a savage breast." It can also soothe your soul, your inner being. It helps enormously to play quiet relaxing music when using some of the intuitive techniques but sometimes you just want music on its own. Play passages you really like. Good music is not written to be played low. Even soft music sounds best at a reasonable volume. (Don't take this though as an excuse to blast you neighbours out of it). Lie back in your favourite armchair or spread out on a couch. Allow the music to envelop you. The onus is on the composer to speak to you through his music, but you must open your being to hear it. If you are fairly exhausted, need relaxing and rejuvenating I know of no better piece than Beethoven's Seventh Symphony.

Interpreting Your Intuitive Thoughts

If you haven't yet done so start an intuition journal. In it you will write down all your intuitive thoughts, ideas and feelings from your relaxation and focusing exercises. Of course, if you just use any of these techniques only once, you may not bother to keep notes but once you experience the exercises and realise how powerful they are, you will find it really worthwhile to keep the journal. Over time, you will notice trends and patterns that will reveal more of yourself to you.

Not keeping a journal is like not recording knowledge as it is discovered. Imagine if previous generations had not recorded their discoveries, thoughts and ideas. So much would be lost and successive generations would be condemned to repeating the same mistakes and reinventing that which had already been discovered. It also signals to your subconscious that you are serious. Trust me, keeping an intuitive journal will be one of the best investments you have ever made.

As you read through newspapers and magazines, cut

out pictures, headlines, articles that catch your eye, especially if they are not in your normal field of interest. Keep these clippings with your journal. Write the date on the back of the piece of newspaper or article. Over time you will notice underlying trends. These trends will recall messages from your subconscious.

There is no precise way to understand your intuitive messages. You have to decide what they mean to you. You will need to read them over and use your logical mind to interpret them. As you go over them, one part may jump out at you and that will be the answer. One image may suggest something completely different, perhaps an association from your childhood, which suggests an activity that is your answer. The main thing is you will know. Your inner being will react and say, "Yes, that's it." As you ponder your notes, just allow the answer to come to you. We will explore this further in the dreaming section of this chapter.

Your mind thinks in pictures and images, not words. If I asked you to close your eyes and describe your bedroom, a picture of that room would appear in your mind's eye. The furniture, curtains, bed linen, would most definitely not be words or letters of the alphabet. Frequently, the images in your mind will bring out certain feelings or emotions in you. An image of a tree in a field may bring a memory of a picnic from years ago – a cherished childhood memory. If someone you knew was struck by lightning while standing under a tree in a thunderstorm, it might bring a totally different emotion. Most often, the images though would be neutral, but they all have a message.

Surely you must have had the experience of talking with someone, and something they said triggered an entirely different thought in your mind? Let's say during the conversation your friend says "flowers" and you say, "That reminds me, I have to pick up my nephew early from school." Explaining to your puzzled friend – "You said 'flowers' – and yesterday I bought a bunch of flowers and was arranging them in a vase when my sister phoned asking if I could pick up my nephew from school."

A Russian Sherlock Holmes

Thoughts and different word associations can lead you down unexplored paths. Here is a fun story, which owes more to logical reasoning than intuitive interpretation, but it does illustrate the point.

A Jewish scholar, living in Russia, wanted to visit Moscow. After much negotiation, which dragged on for months, he was granted permission. Boarding the train, he found a seat in an empty compartment. At the next station, a young man entered the compartment and sat down.

The scholar looked at the young man and thought: "Well, he doesn't look like a peasant but he probably comes from this district. Now this is a Jewish district so therefore he must be Jewish. On the other hand, I am the only one from our district who has permission to go to Moscow, so where could this man be going? Ah, just outside Moscow there is a little village called Samvet, and you don't require special permission to visit there.

But why is he going to Samvet? He must be going to visit one of the Jewish families there but now there are only two. The Bernsteins and the Steinbergs. The Bernsteins are a pretty nasty bunch, so he must be visiting the Steinbergs.

But why? The Steinbergs have only girls, so maybe he is their son-in-law. But if so, which daughter did he marry? Sarah married the nice lawyer from Budapest and Rebecca married a businessman from Zamodir, so it must be Sarah's husband. Now if I am not mistaken, his name is Alexander Cohen. But he comes from Budapest, they are very anti-Semitic there, so he must have changed his name. What's the Hungarian equivalent of Cohen? Kovacs! But if they let him change his name, he must have some special status. What could it be? A doctorate from the university."

At this point the scholar turns to his fellow traveller and

says, "How do you do, Dr Kovacs?" "Very well, thank you," declared the surprised passenger, "but how do you happen to know my name?" "Oh," replied the scholar, "it was obvious."

Let the Images Flow

After you have asked your question which might be, "Where did grandpa hide the will?" allow images to flow through your mind, one thing leading to another, sometimes logically, more often not.

If one image, say a car, comes into your mind and does not seem to offer the answer, ask yourself aloud, "I see a car, what does that mean to me?" And continue aloud. Let us say in response to the question, "Where did grandpa hide the will?" the image of a car does come into your mind. The car, as you allow your mind to wander, you see is towing a caravan, which reminds you of a lot of colourful caravans, which reminds you of a circus, which leads you to animals, leading you to an elephant with a big trunk. Yes, that's it. The big trunk in the attic – that's where the will is.

Use any or all of these methods as you need them. Mix them up and choose the techniques that suit you best. They will empower you.

Dreaming and Sleeping

"Have You Ever Seen a Letter from Your Subconscious?"

Sleep Stupidity

On March 25th 1997 the 3,000-tonne container ship *Cita*, crashed into the Scilly Isles, foundering on rocks off St Mary's Island. The eight-man crew were rescued by helicopter and a few days later the ship broke up and sank.

The marine accident investigation branch found that all eight crew members, including the Mate, who had been officially on watch, were asleep. Statutory law insists on ten hours' rest in every twenty-four and the work schedule of this ship certainly didn't allow for this. The previous night the Mate had been supervising loading at Southampton. He had three hours' sleep in the early afternoon the previous day, and three more before taking the midnight watch. Being in no fit state to take over his duties, the enquiry found it was no wonder he fell asleep.

Other modern disasters are also sleep related. The nuclear meltdown at Chernobyl, the nuclear fallout at Three Mile Island, the Challenger Space Shuttle explosion, all had sleepy people making bad decisions at critical moments. According to Dr Stanley Coren, a neuropsychologist at the University of British Columbia, Canada, the faulty O-ring seals were not the real cause of the space shuttle disaster – "in NASA's rush to make itself economically independent, ground personnel had been working 14-hour shifts for up to 26 days straight at a time. The engineers had warned early on that the O-ring seals were suspect, but the program schedulers were just too out of it to register the problem. The real cause was sleep stupidity."

How Much Sleep Do You Need?

Lack of sleep, especially over a few days, will adversely affect your rational mind, your reflex actions as well as putting your body functions out of kilter. Laboratory tests show that your IQ will diminish with each hour of less sleep than the norm. If you can get a good night's sleep the following night, the balance will redress itself. But if you continue with a series of late nights, the diminishing of your IQ will accumulate and after a week you will be borderline retarded and about as useful as a drunken driver. Adequate sleep is also vital for our subconscious minds and our dreams.

There are two basic kinds of sleep, slow wave deep sleep (SWS) that for the most part occurs during the first half of the night and rapid eye movement (REM) when dreams occur.

Laboratory tests in America allowed the subjects to have uninterrupted normal SWS sleep but did not allow them to drift into the REM state. After one day, they showed signs of irritability, after forty-eight hours they were very irritated and short tempered. After seventy-two hours of normal sleep, but no REM sleep, they started to become extremely nervous and volatile. The tests were discontinued for fear the participants would develop ongoing personality disorders. Allowing the volunteers regular sleep with REM, within forty-eight hours they were almost back to normal.

In more recent tests at Harvard Medical School, researchers found that a good night's sleep will make you up to forty per cent measurably smarter than you were the day before. The evidence suggests that adequate REM sleep is crucial to memory formation and learning. Rats had to find their way through a maze – learning a new skill. At the end of the day, it was noted what they had learned. That night, they had longer than normal amounts of REM sleep. The next day, their learning had improved up to forty per cent. Other rats, deprived of REM, showed considerably less, or no improvement. All this suggests that during REM, new messages are being planted on the brain cells, resulting in improved learning. If you have practiced visualisation, you will understand the similarities. You are smarter the next day because your mind has been rehearsing during the night.

Incidentally, you should never leave minor tasks such as washing the dishes undone at night. Your mind knows you will have to do them in the morning and will be rehearsing dishes all night. Don't clutter your mind with such unnecessary drivel. Allow it to focus on worthwhile things.

If you found a large pile of coins, some gold, some silver and some copper and you could take all you could carry, which ones would you fill your pockets with? Gold coins are worth many times more than silver and they in turn are valued much higher than copper. They each take up as much space as the other and weigh about the same. It only takes as much effort to pick up a gold coin as a copper or silver one. Go for the gold. Deposit only golden ideas in your mind. Your mind will return solid gold to you.

What Your Dreams Are Telling You

Dream sleep also has even greater advantages. It can reveal to you the answers to problems, your inner worries, the right decisions to make – dreams are memos to yourself. Jung insisted that dreams and their analysis properly belonged to the dreamer as a rich source of personal experience, insight, even genius.

Our civilisation is resplendent with well-documented stories of artists, writers, musicians and businessmen using the visions and insights from their dreams to help guide them with their creative efforts. Listen, if these guys and gals paid attention to their dreams and the results led to creativity and money, shouldn't you be paying attention too?

Creative Dreamers

Conrad Hilton, founder of the international chain of hotels bearing his name, regularly used his hunches and dreams for decision-making. He called them his "invisible counsellors". Once, tendering for the Steevens Corporation, his sealed bid was for $165,000. The following morning, the number $180,000 was swirling around in his mind. He felt it was the way to go and upped his bid to that amount. He got the company and later sold it for $2m profit. As it turned out, the under bidder was $179,800 – only $200 less than Hilton's.

Punch and Judy performer Eric Sharp was trying to figure out a way to make his puppet booth more portable. The concept was on his mind for months. He woke at three in the morning with the answer. He immediately wrote it down with plans and sketches. Two days later he had built the prototype. The booth could be assembled or dismantled in ten seconds, stood eight foot high, folded down to the size of a large suitcase and could be carried over the shoulder, leaving both hands free. This was a major improvement when you realise the normal puppet booth takes five to ten minutes to assemble.

Samuel Taylor Coleridge dreamed the poem *Kubla Kahn* and awoke with it entirely in his head. He got up to write it down, and did so until a friend called. When Coleridge went back – the rest of the poem was gone. "It had passed away like the images on a stream into which a stone has been cast."

During the American Civil War, an acquaintance suggested to Julia Ward Howe that she could write better lyrics to the song *John Brown's Body*. She had often felt the need herself for better words. It's interesting that an outsider suggesting what you already know is the force that sets off the reaction.

Early the following morning she awoke with the words, "Mine eyes have seen the glory of the coming of the Lord …" She was intelligent enough not to push the creative process and lay there in the still of the morning allowing the words to come to her. Only when the lyrics were complete and her inner voice was still, did she get out of bed and write it all down. Returning to bed she said to herself, "I like this better than most things I have written." She dozed off and upon reawakening could not recall any of the words at all. Fortunately she had written them down.

Write It Down

I mentioned this earlier and it is worth repeating. You will awaken with a brilliant idea. You will hardly believe that you came up with something so good. In fact, it will be so good and sometimes so obvious, that you just know you will remember it in the morning, and besides you are too comfortable in bed to get up. I promise you this, if you don't get up straight away and write it down, and doze off thinking it's such a wonderful idea you will remember it in the morning, that when you do wake up in the morning, you will remember that you had a brilliant idea but you will not remember for the life of you what it was. I know – it has happened to me. More than once. I have learned my lesson! Get up and write it down. If you don't, your inner mind will see that you are not serious about the brilliant ideas it gives you and it will switch off and not bother. When it sees you are serious it will give you more and better ideas.

The Riddle of the Disappearing Van

Your dreams can also reveal an inner fear, one you may not consciously be aware of. When I was busy as a magician, frequently doing two or three shows a day, reliable transport was imperative. This would occasionally manifest itself in my dreams, not as my van breaking down but rather it being stolen.

I recall one very vivid dream. The van went missing. Presumably stolen. Being thorough and logical, I informed the police and the insurance company, as well as organising a replacement vehicle which was to be delivered the following morning. When I awoke, I did not realise I had been dreaming, and accepted the whole affair as fact. After breakfast, I was literally stunned when I went out of the front door to find my van parked happily outside where I had left it the night before! It took me a few moments to grasp that it was all … just a dream.

All tradesmen and professionals have a similar common theme running through their dreams. Airline pilots dream they are running out of fuel and can't find the runway to land. Lawyers dream of turning up in court with vital documents missing. Students turn up for an important exam having prepared the wrong questions.

Dream Symbols

Dreams are frequently symbolic. Usually the images will reveal clues to a problem you have been diligently working on beforehand. James Watt worked long and hard on how to make engine parts rotate smoothly. He dreamt of molten metal fragments falling from the sky, and forming into globes as they cooled. This led to the manufacture of ball bearings.

Elias Howe spent several years inventing the sewing machine. One small detail was the stumbling block. One night he dreamt he was captured by a tribe of savages. The leader insisted he finish his invention or be killed. As he was being led away he noticed the spears carried by the savages had eye-shaped holes near the flattened points. When he awoke he made a needle with a hole nearer the point, rather than in the middle. This was the final piece of the puzzle and the basis of the chain-stitch sewing machine.

Interpreting Your Dream

Many books on dreams will tell you that falling means one thing, a lion means another and flying means something else. There is no one simple solution or way of translating dreams that suits everyone – no more than your shoe will fit your neighbour.

Fritz Pearls, the founder of Gestalt Therapy, developed an excellent method of dream interpretation. If you appear in the dream, ask yourself how you feel. What are your perceptions, your emotions, your thoughts?

Next, place yourself in the position of all the other people in the dream. Ask yourself how they feel. Who is speaking? Whose voice is it? What are they saying? Next, place yourself in the position of any animals or living creatures in the dream. What are their feelings? What are they conveying? Finally, place yourself in the position of any inanimate objects in the dream, trees, buildings, bridges etc. Feel yourself in their position. How do they feel and what are they trying to convey?

The Eight Steps to Successful Dreaming

1. Tell yourself before you go to bed that you will remember your dreams.
2. Before you go to bed, ask yourself the question you want the solution for. Be as specific and concise as possible.
3. Keep your dream journal, which can also be your intuition journal, beside your bed. This ensures that your subconscious will take you seriously.
4. You shouldn't take any stimulants for a couple of hours before bed. These could be things like tea, coffee or various other nightcaps. Take a relaxing soak in a hot bath to relieve any physical tension. Baroque music in the background (but not too loud) would help.
5. Before retiring, if you have the time, briefly record your day's activities, especially record thoughts on your feelings about these activities. Write down the question you are asking yourself.
6. Just before you get into the bed, tell yourself that you will sleep soundly, awaken refreshed and that you will remember your dream.
7. When you do wake up, access your mind to retrieve the images from your dream. All you need is one small clue and that will give you the whole dream. It will lead you right through the rest of the dream.
8. Record your dream in your journal or onto a tape recorder.

Now you have to interpret what you have. Unravel the strands or blow away the clouds. Give your dream a title, as though it were a book. Use as few words as possible. What is the theme of your dream? Again, use as few words as possible. Maximum – one sentence. What are the major symbols in your dream? What seems to stick out most in your mind? Is it hiding something? What are your feelings? Using the exercises in the intuition section, discover what word, image or associations you can follow. Using logic, decide what it means. You will know when you have the right answer.

CHAPTER 10

Stacking the Dice in Your Favour

We are creatures of habit. Over time we have developed our set ways of doing things. The way you get up, when you wash, what you have for breakfast, when you leave for the office and the route you take. At work you will tend to park in the same spot or the same area of the car park. You will either drive face in or you will reverse in. Through years of performing at private parties in people's homes, I would always park facing the gate. If other guests arrived after me, I might find it very difficult otherwise to reverse out. To this day, if I perceive a potential difficulty in driving away afterwards, I will reverse the car in.

The habits we develop form the safety barriers of our comfort zones. They are, "at the edge of the envelope". That phrase comes from the test pilots, testing new models of planes. The first day the pilot will take the plane so high and so fast. That is the present edge of the envelope, or the comfort zone for that plane. Next day, he will go higher and faster, expanding the edge of the envelope. This continues until the plane can travel no higher or faster without serious problems. This is the outer edge of the envelope for that plane.

Very few people make the effort to get out of their comfort zone or to expand their envelope. While there is a limit to how fast and how high any plane can go, psychologists believe that our own mental potential as humans is virtually limitless.

Into the Mind Zone

The steps covered in this chapter will not directly make you more intuitive. What they will do is teach you to think beyond the comfort zone. By opening your mind to experiencing new things or approaching existing routines from a new angle, you are telling your subconscious that it is okay to be open to new ways. Your mind is therefore encouraged to view new experiences positively and the deeper message is to be more accepting of that which is not the norm. In so doing, you are indirectly opening your own intuitive powers and processes.

You are training yourself that there is more than one way of achieving a goal. After a while your mind will automatically look at problems or decisions from different angles. You will have developed the habit and start perceiving ideas that are unseen by others. Because your mind is no longer conditioned to seeing things "in the comfort zone" it will see the bigger picture.

How Do You Get Up In The Morning?

Start off with how you get up in the morning. This is fun and it works. Whatever you want to do the next day, programme yourself the night before. In his book *See You At the Top*, Zig Ziglar suggests telling yourself before going to bed, "When the alarm clock goes off, I will sit straight up in bed and say, 'It's a great day to get up and get at them.' "

I tried this and it really works. You may get some very funny looks from your spouse – especially if you haven't explained what you are doing!

You can, as I have, take it further. Let's start off with Zig's idea. You are also going to train yourself to initiate new experiences. So you will exit the bed on a different side. It might be the other side of the bed, or the end of the bed. If you dress from the top down, start dressing from the bottom up. If you put on your right shoe first, start with your left foot (in your left shoe of course).

There is always something you need to do every day and it is usually the thing you keep putting off. It might be writing letters or doing your daily exercise. Brian Tracy calls it "swallowing the frog". A group of executives have a difficult decision to make. Someone produces a box of small frogs and the executives get one each. They have to swallow their frog. The thought alone is repulsive but the executives do it, and everything after that is easy. The most difficult thing has been gotten out of the way. They have swallowed the frog. Your frog might be that important letter, the taxes or a report. By doing it first you have put the most difficult task of the day behind you and all the rest is plain sailing.

Right then, before you go to bed, take thirty seconds to programme yourself for the next day. Your instructions to yourself might read: "When the clock sounds off in the morning, I will sit straight up in bed saying it's a great day to get up and get at them. I will climb out of the end of the bed. I will dress myself starting with my socks and I see myself having completed my tax return." One other thing – you must visualise this entire scene happening in your mind.

Experiment with Different Foods

Experience something new for breakfast. If you always breakfast at home, eat out once in a while. As most people are not fully alert first thing in the morning it is easier to programme new ideas. Sample different kinds of cereal, fresh fruit, yoghurt, muesli or a cooked breakfast. Do this at least once a week and on a different day each week. Carry this over into your other meals. If eating out and you don't feel adventurous enough to try a new main course, then order a different starter.

Travel to Work by Different Routes

Going to work a different way will give you a new awareness of your environment. You will discover roads you didn't know existed. You will pass by businesses whose services you will use. Better still, you may find a new company you can do business with. If you always drive, take the bus or train. In Dublin we have double-decker buses, that is a bus with an upstairs. You would be amazed at the different perspective you get from the top of a bus, especially if it takes a route you think you know well.

Magazines

Marketing genius Jay Abraham conducted this exercise at one of his seminars I attended in 1996. He gave us all a magazine in an area in which we had no particular interest. A keen golfer might get a magazine on knitting, or a middle-aged lady might get one on bodybuilding. You get the idea. The object of the exercise was to pick a section of the magazine and find something that related to the marketing lessons studied that day. We were to report back in the morning. At the time I thought it was daft (which also shows how adults do not automatically welcome new experiences). However, I was committed to giving it a go. I opened my magazine at random and read two paragraphs. I found two points, which were directly relevant to my business. I opened to another page and thought – nothing here. I re-scanned the page and one word hit me, which suggested another word in my mind, which solved another problem, which had nothing to do with marketing. Other delegates had equally positive results. For your next plane journey, buy a magazine at the airport; one you would normally never buy. Allow it to speak to you.

The Seminar

Most business seminars start at a set time in the morning and finish up at about 5pm. Not Jay Abraham. His three-day seminars start each morning at 8.30 and can go on until midnight or longer. He asked delegates to suspend their view of what a seminar should be like. Many found this challenging. But there truly was method in his madness. After a certain period of time your conscious mind rebels and closes down. It cannot take in and process any more information. But your subconscious mind is taking it all in. Because Jay's seminars are not cheap and most of the delegates are business owners they have all made a serious commitment to be there. With your subconscious on overdrive, the positive expectation of your fellow delegates and Jay's masterful strategies, a synergy develops that yields meaningful insights for you and your business.

Your Word Power

Your ability to communicate and express yourself determines your salary. Look at any organisation and you will see that the leaders are the better communicators. Here is my suggestion. When you come across a new word, or a word you aren't really sure about, look it up in the dictionary. Check it out also in the thesaurus and find words with the same meaning. Each new word you learn will therefore bring two or three new words into your active vocabulary. It will also help you think clearer and more concisely.

The Boomerang Principle

Give good to the universe without expecting anything in return. Helping other people who cannot help you, such as teaching an illiterate person to read does wonders for your self-esteem. By putting good out into the universe, like planting a tree you will never get to see mature, you are opening doorways for wonderful and unforeseen things to come your way. You never know where an act of kindness may lead.

The Boomerang Returns

In the late 1800s, an English statesman was travelling up through Scotland for an important occasion. His coach became stuck in the mud. A farm boy gathered some horses and pulled him out. The young man would accept no payment. He was happy to be of assistance. The Englishman asked if there was anything the boy aspired to. He wanted to be a doctor. The statesman said he would help with his education.

More than half a century later, another English statesman, Winston Churchill, lay seriously ill with pneumonia when he was given a new drug called penicillin, which cured him. Alexander Fleming was the developer of this drug. He was also the farm boy who pulled Randolph Churchill's carriage out of the mud. Randolph was Winston Churchill's father. You never know!! Expect good things to happen and you will attract good things into your life.

You Become What You Think About

Our minds lead us in the direction of our dominant thoughts. You really do attract what you expect and think about. Napoleon Hill, author of the all-time best-selling classic, *Think and Grow Rich* put it this way: "You become what you think about." If your passion is juggling and each day you are thinking about it, practising and working on new ways of improving your skills, you cannot but excel at juggling. And the same with any field of interest. However, thinking positive thoughts alone will get you nowhere. You need to combine it with positive, enthusiastic action.

***"Affirmation without discipline leads to delusion."* Jim Rohn**

My Most Embarrassing Experience

Back in 1972 I read an interesting trick in a magicians' magazine. Part of the secret device that enabled the trick to work was a strong, flexible, waterproof container. In this case it was a condom. At the time I was planning a cabaret act and I felt the effect in the magazine would be a highlight of the show. There was a snag. Condoms were not available in Ireland. They were banned. It was illegal to import, distribute or sell them. At that time, the word condom was not even mentioned in polite company. Now, times have definitely changed.

So I had no way of learning the trick. Until, two years later, Eric and Muriel Sharp invited me over to study magic and learn Punch and Judy. They lived outside a small village called Pontyclun in South Wales. I knew the devices were available from chemist shops. I had heard from my friends that they came in different sizes and colours. So I decided to splash out £5, which was a lot at the time, and purchase a wide assortment. I also figured that there would be enough to last for lots of shows. At the time, another magician from Dublin, who did a clever manipulative act, suffered from dry hands. Hearing I was going to Wales, he asked me to buy a tube of Glymiel jelly, as it was a great antidote to the dryness. Jars of it sold in

Ireland but he wanted it in a tube as it was just easier to carry and less likely to get broken.

So, one morning, I wandered down to the village and found a very modern chemist's shop. I was a skinny eighteen year old, looking younger than my years. I decided that I would not be embarrassed. I kept saying to myself, "I will not be embarrassed!" over and over.

It was a long shop and I walked right up to the counter. There were two attractive girls slightly older than I was, serving. I looked one of them right in the eye and said, "I want £5 worth of assorted condoms please!" as if I were buying sweets. The girls were slightly taken aback, when a man's face appeared through a hatch behind them. The pharmacist. "I'll look after this, girls," he said.

He came down and took a plain brown paper bag. We walked to the centre of the store and there was a large display rack of condoms. Now I was surprised. It had never dawned on me that they would be on open display. I had assumed they would be hidden behind the counter.

The pharmacist was very helpful. "Perhaps sir would like some of these, and these." I nodded as he filled up the bag. I decided not to tell him why I really wanted them, secretly hoping I might be perceived of as a macho stud surrounded by attractive girls all fighting for my attention. The total came to £5.13 and he generously only charged me the £5 I had allocated. I thanked him and left the shop.

As soon as I closed the door, I remembered the jelly for the hands. Back in I go. The pharmacist had disappeared behind the hatch. I faced the two girls. "A tube of Glymiel jelly, please." They looked at me, at each other, and burst out laughing. I went bright red. All the embarrassment I was avoiding cloaked me with a vengeance. "It's not for me, it's for a friend," I pleaded. They roared. I went crimson. In a vain effort to extricate myself, I explained, "It's for rubbing on your hands before performing." One of them howled and had tears running down her cheeks. Oh, how I wanted the floor to open and swallow me. I realised I was in a pit with no escape. I stopped digging. Mercifully, the pharmacist re-appeared, and trying to keep a straight face, supplied me with the jelly and I departed slightly comforted by the fact I would never have to enter that shop again.

The lesson here is that I was focused on not being embarrassed - a negative thought and I attracted more of it than I ever want again. It's like the football coach who says to the player about to take a penalty shot, "Don't aim for the top right." What happens? He shoots for the top right and the 'keeper saves the shot. The top right was the dominant thought. "Aim low left," would have been the better suggestion. Plant the thought of what you do want, not what you do not want.

I Give Myself Permission To Use Affirmations

Affirmations are another way of bringing positive expectation into your life. Texas sales and negotiating trainer Barney Zick has a great one: "I got money coming." Say that aloud, five times every morning with meaning. Simple affirmations are:

- *Something wonderful will happen today.*
- *I trust my intuition.*
- *I like myself.*
- *I am a great salesman (or plumber, manager, whatever you do).*
- *I feel terrific (said with vigour and emotion, you will fee much better no matter what your current state).*
- *I give myself permission to be powerful.*
- *I am a genius.* If you doubt you can operate on genius level reread Chapter 3. Inwardly you may not

believe you are a genius. Keep saying the affirmation, "I am a genius." One day, unexpectedly you will say something in conversation. The person you are talking to will say, "Wow, that's clever. How did you come up with that?" Just smile inwardly and say to yourself, "Well of course, I am a genius."

Laugh It Off

Barney Zick has an unusual sense of humour. He will enter a busy elevator on the ground floor and press floors 1 and 2. He will stand with his back to the doors facing the people. As the doors close he will start talking to the crowd, "I bet you are wondering why I called you all here today?" When the elevator reaches the first floor, he will step out, secretly and swiftly climb the stairs to the second floor. When the doors of the elevator open he will smile at the people, saying, "You were talking about me."

Sometimes if stopped at traffic lights a motorist may not realise the lights have changed in his favour. A friendly toot of the horn from the car following can be a helpful reminder. Occasionally the driver behind becomes quite agitated and impatient. A more aggressive "honk honk" says, "Get the heck out of my way, you moron. Can't you see the lights are green?" In this situation, Barney has been known to get out of his auto and approach the car behind. He is six feet four inches tall and built like the Terminator. He saunters towards the offending vehicle with a Texas cowboy stroll. He bends down to the driver and smiles sweetly. "Thank you so much for that friendly reminder. So many people today think only of themselves. There was I, lost in thought and through your kindness I was reminded that there are other road users and I was blocking their path. Thank you so much for your consideration." By this time they are speechless and the lights have changed back to red. Barney's message – "There is too much fun to be had to take life too seriously."

How Long Do You Plan to Live?

As I write, the life expectancy for men is mid-seventies and for women, touching eighty. With more awareness about food, nutrition and exercise, and the major advances in medicine, predictions are that this will increase dramatically. My grandfather on my mother's side lived to be eighty-one, as did my father. Both were smokers. So, I figured that I should last at least as long, barring accidents. I don't smoke and am not a drinker. Still I figured about eighty-one.

At what age do you plan to die? Most people have a figure in mind when they think they are likely to pop off. Let us say it is also eighty-one. How do you see yourself at eighty – the year before you expect to die? In good health or riddled with illness? Fairly fit? Your mental faculties working well? Physically active? Financially secure? If you visualise yourself in good condition isn't it feasible that you could live a few years longer, maybe five, ten or fifteen years longer? If you could what would you do during those extra years? What would you accomplish? Where would you visit? Who would you meet? Wouldn't these things be important to you?

If they are, why aren't you doing them now?

You may think living so much longer is a bit far-fetched. Recently I heard an interview with Alexander Everett, who has decided to live to be 120. He feels if the oldest people on earth can live to that age, why shouldn't he? Interesting thought!

At the age of 104 Walt Jones's wife died. Walt, of Tacoma, Washington, bought a motor home and drove all over the US visiting forty-three States. A year later he sold his properties and invested the money, which would bring him in a good monthly income. At the age of 110, on the Johnny Carson TV show, he said he had earned more money in the last five years than in all the years previously. He started dating a woman in her sixties!

Grandma Moses started painting in her seventies and had an exhibition in a top New York gallery at the age of

100. She developed a new art form known as "Primitive American".

So, how long do you plan to live? If you plan to live to be 120 and don't make it, you may still well live longer than you would have otherwise. Because if you expect to live to be 120, your body and mind will work towards that expectation and guide you towards taking better care of yourself.

> ***"If I had known I was going to live this long, I would have taken better care of myself."*** **Phil Harris**

Can You See Beyond Your Nose?

Psychologists did some experiments with four-year-old schoolchildren. A child would be in a room with an adult. The adult would put a sweet on the table and explain that he was just going for a message. When he left, the child could have the sweet, but if the child didn't eat it and waited until the adult returned, the child could have the sweet plus a second one.

About eighty per cent of the children ate the sweet while the adult was away, and twenty per cent waited and claimed the second one. Following the children through school, the twenty per cent who were prepared to wait did better academically. From an early age they somehow perceived the value of an investment and how over time it could benefit them.

The least well-off people in our society are the ones who only see one day at a time. Manual labourers generally live in the present. They do not see the value of long-term investment in themselves or in a business. Managers and professional people tend more to focus on the future and have goals. They understand the law of sowing and reaping and that they don't both happen in the same season. Remember, plant the seed and the universe will give you the tree.

The Takers and the Givers

Be very careful with whom you associate. If you hang around with losers, you yourself will be a loser. Hang around with winners and you too will be a winner.

If you play tennis with people equally or less skilled than you, you will not, cannot, improve. Play with a better player and you will have to improve just to stay in the game.

The winners in life understand that you have to give before you get, the losers want to take before they give – if they would ever give at all. It is like going to a stove demanding, "Give me heat!" Sorry, you have to put in fuel and light the fire. That is the effort. Once started, the fire keeps going with minimal maintenance. It is the law of sowing and reaping. Notice again the sowing comes before the reaping.

So it is with developing intuition. With most people it is buried under logical reasoning, the influence of others and a fear of the unknown. By following the suggestions in this book, you will be uncovering and releasing your intuition. You will be giving it a freer rein, and by acting on its flashes and inspirations, you will encourage it to be more active in your life. You must follow your hunches, your inner voice. If you don't, your inner being will feel ignored and cease to provide you with useful guidance. The more you use your intuition, the more encouraged it will feel and the more it will benefit you.

Change

A Buddhist monk visiting New York goes to a hotdog stand and says, "Make me one with everything."

Tending $5 for the $1 hotdog he queries why he doesn't get his $4 back. The vendor's reply: "Change has to come from within."

Me and My Life

Everybody has taken over something.

The Irish Language.
Poetry.
Anything to do with James Joyce.
The Arts.
Theatre.

Everybody has taken over something.
They think they own it.

They will keep you in your place.

You must go to them
through them
be cleared by them
approved by them
sanctioned by them
get permission from them.

Most of the time this works
because people desperately want
something from them.

mostly money, grants, cnuas,
call it what you will,
dangle it on a stick
and they will dance.

Everybody has taken over something.
They think they own it.

I do not need them
so
they don't own me.

Pat Ingoldsby

CHAPTER 11

The Owners of Truth

***"What has been believed by all always and everywhere has every likelihood of being untrue."* (Paul Valery)**

The old Rabbi was on his deathbed. Regarded as a wise and holy man by his rabbinical students, they gathered around him for some words of wisdom. His top student said, "Master, we know your time has come and we will miss you. Are there any words of comfort and wisdom you can leave with us? What is the meaning of life?" The old man thought for a few moments and said, "Life is like a barrel of water."

The student passed the words of wisdom down the line to the other scholars until it reached the least academic pupil. "Life is like a barrel of water," he was told. "But what exactly does it mean?" he asked. "I don't know," came the reply. "Well, ask him before he dies," said the dim one, "I need to know what he means."

So the question passes up to the number one student. "What exactly does the Rabbi mean, life is like a barrel of water?" "It's obvious," said the bright student, "he means that sometimes the barrel is full, sometimes it is drained. Life is the same. Sometimes there is great energy and sometimes we are tired and listless. Sometimes the water is clear; sometimes it's muddy. So too with life. Sometimes we know where we are going and other times we are going around in circles, getting nowhere. We make no progress. The water can be used to help plants grow. So too with life. We sow what we reap. Tell him that's what the Master means."

The interpretation was passed along the line to the last and dimmest student. "I don't want to know what that clever clogs thinks he means, I want to know exactly what the Rabbi means. Ask him. Tell him to ask the Rabbi." Again the request gets passed up the line.

Somewhat exasperated, the top student turns to the Rabbi and he says "Master, I am so sorry to trouble you, but the dull one here wants to know what exactly do you mean by life is like a barrel of water?" The old man gathers all his strength, shrugs his shoulders and his last words are, "So it isn't like a barrel of water."

There is a lot to be learned from this story. It is so easy for someone in authority to make a pronouncement and have it accepted as gospel. Many will accept an erroneous belief as dogma. Cults can grow and develop. Political parties can flourish. Religious doctrines can spring up and spread. Entire philosophies of life can result. The consequences can be more devastating than a plague. The moral is just because someone says something, does it mean it's true? Just because you read it in the paper or you read it in a book does not mean it's true. And if it is true, it may only apply to certain circumstances and not all circumstances. Likewise, do not accept what I am saying just because I am saying it. Maybe I am wrong. My point is, not to accept as truth or dogma the teachings or preachings of others without question. Put it through your filtering system and ask yourself, "Is this true for me? Does this apply to me?"

> ***"Faced with the choice of changing one's mind or proving there is no need to do so, most people get busy with the proof." –* J.K. Galbraith**

It seems to be an inherent trait in human nature to show how we can't do something. Even if the potential gains promise great rewards. Consider these phrases:

- Maintaining the status quo.
- Leave things as they are.
- Don't rock the boat.
- That's the way we have always done it here.
- We tried that and it didn't work.

What about Og, the guy who invented the wheel? What kind of abuse did he have to put up with? "Yeah," you can imagine his friends saying, "real men carry the heavy stuff. Wheels are for wimps." We become fixated by routine and the way we have always done things. And yet, there would have been no improvements in the life of man were it not for change and innovation. There are two types of change, major and minor.

Major and Minor Changes

Major change is the most difficult for people to encounter and contemplate. This is a whole new way of doing things that they have been doing on a regular basis. In the 1960s, after the Second Vatican Council, the Catholic Church decided to do away with the Latin mass. Instead, mass would be celebrated in the language spoken by the people of that particular country. This created major controversy and more than three decades later, many still long for the old ways.

There are strong views that women should be able to be ordained. There are equally vociferous views that they should not and could not be. They say if Jesus felt that there should be women priests, he would have picked them himself. If you apply that logic, then all priests and ministers should be Palestinian Jewish fishermen!

But look at a change that Jesus made. All priests in the Jewish religion at that time came from the tribe of Levi – the Levites. Coming from a different lineage, Jesus claimed that he himself was a priest, an idea that was blasphemous at the time and turned the authorities against him. This was part of a chain of events that led to his death. He challenged the accepted traditions of his time. He was not prepared to accept the status quo. He did not shy away from controversy. He questioned standards and beliefs. Above all he was true to himself in everything he did.

The Invention That Made the Motorcar Possible

The motorcar would not have been made possible, as Henry Ford agreed, if the pneumatic tyres had not been invented.

John Boyd Dunlop developed the pneumatic tyre, as we know it today. The original bicycles had solid rubber tyres and they made heavy work of short journeys and endurance tests of long distance runs. Even cycling around the streets was a jarring experience. Dunlop wondered about making the wheels lighter and he thought about this on and off for years. In 1887 he inflated a rubber tube and attached it to a wooden wheel. This basic contraption was far from perfect but it worked. He ordered a bicycle to be made up with the device but its first outing drew howls of derision from all the passers-by, workmen and tradesmen! It was equally derided when it had its first outing on the streets of London. But slowly it caught on, made bicycle travelling easier, simpler and more pleasurable and, as mentioned earlier, helped make the motorcar possible.

Minor changes tend to be embraced more easily. For example, washing machines, as we know them today have many different programmes on them, some up to thirty or forty possibilities. And yet, I don't know anyone who has ever used more than three settings on their washing machine. Still, many people will feel that unless they have all the programmes, they won't be with it or up to date.

Women in Space

A few years ago, Lieutenant-Colonel Eileen Collins was the first woman to pilot a space shuttle, the *Discovery*. Why did it take so long to put a woman at the helm of an American spaceship?

As the space age dawned in the late 1950s, the United States embarked on a project called "MISS" (man in space soonest). Hundreds of men were subjected to a programme of physical and psychological tests that were described by some as sadistic torture. Only seven passed, and they went on to become the astronauts of Project Mercury.

As the Mercury capsule was very small, someone had the bright idea of testing a group of women. Women are generally smaller than men, consume less food and oxygen and are less susceptible to heart attacks, monotony, loneliness, heat, cold, pain and noise. "And anyway," observed one woman candidate, "there were women on the *Mayflower* and on the first wagon trains, so why not in space?"

Twenty-five women were tested and the results were astounding: thirteen of them passed, some of them ahead of the male candidates. They rode exercise bikes to exhaustion, swallowed a metre-long rubber hose, drank radioactive water and were prodded, tilted and spun until they couldn't stand. The most sadistic test became known as the "dog dip".

Each candidate was submerged blindfolded in a tank of body temperature water in a soundproofed and darkened room, so that she was blind and deaf with no sense of touch, taste or smell. This could produce horrifying effects. One male subject heard dogs barking, sang obscene songs, wept over the state of humanity and cried out for inner voices to be silent. No man lasted more than three hours in this ultimate test of nerves under stress. Yet, some of the women floated serenely in the tank for ten hours. The testers concluded that the thirteen women should go forward for further tests.

Two days before these tests were to begin, however, the programme was suddenly cancelled. Why? One reason given was because none of the women aviators was an experienced jet fighter pilot, so they could not be qualified to be astronauts. A NASA spokesman was heard to say, "Talk of an American spacewoman makes me sick to my stomach." Yet the real reason that women were cancelled from the space programme was that the Americans were committed to putting a man in space.

Fewer than two per cent of the men tested passed and yet over fifty per cent of the women tested passed. In spite of overwhelming evidence, the blind misogyny of the status quo remained.

Who Else Wants Time-Saving Methods?

In the 1940's memory expert Harry Lorayne developed a system to memorise the Morse code, which is made up of a series of dots and dashes. By allowing the letter "R" to stand for and represent the dot, and the letter "T" represent the dash, he was able to put together a series of words which would remind him of the code signal for a particular letter.

For example, the letter A is made up of a dot and a dash, so a dot is represented by R and a dash by the letter T. Putting R and T together comes up with the word "RaT".

The letter B is dash, dot, dot, dot, so we have to find a T, and three R's. So he came up with the word "TeRRoR".

The letter C is made up of a dash, a dot, a dash and a dot, so that is TRTR, and he came up with the word "ToRTuRe", and so on.

To help him remember what letter went with each (A went with rat), you would think of "Amazing Rat". B goes with terror – you would have "Blind Terror". C goes with torture, so "Cold Torture".

Using this method and going through the rest of the alphabet, you could easily memorise the Morse code in thirty minutes to an hour. Of course, it would take considerably longer to become proficient in using it but you would have at least learned what the dots and dashes meant for each letter.

In the Signals section of the American army, soldiers took six months to learn the Morse code. Three months to learn what dots and dashes went with each letter and then three months practising to become proficient in sending messages. Harry contacted the commander in charge and said he could teach the men how to use the Morse code in half a day. In other words, the first three months of training could be condensed into one afternoon. His offer was declined because he was told, "We have set aside six months for them to learn, three to train and three to practice and if they learned it in one afternoon, well what would we do with the rest of three months – sorry, we can't use you."

The Trappings of Power

Up to the 1800s seafaring was a risky way of making a living. It wasn't easy to plot your exact position on the globe. Experienced navigators could accurately predict the latitudes – distance from the equator. The longitudes – the distance east or west from Greenwich – were considerably more difficult. Bad weather could easily mean the calculations of the most seasoned mariners were nothing more than guesswork. Even a small error could set a ship off course and onto rocks.

Such was the scene on October 22nd 1707. Admiral Sir Clowdisley Shovell and his fleet of five ships were returning to England from skirmishes with the French forces near Gibraltar. After twelve foggy days at sea, he feared for the safety of his ships. There was potential danger from foundering on coastal rocks. He assembled all his navigators and the unanimous opinion placed them safely west of Ile de Ouessant, near Brittany. Unfortunately for them, they were in fact very close to the Scilly Isles, off the coast of Cornwall.

A sailor on the flagship, the *Association*, approached the officers. He had secretly kept his own personal log and he calculated that the ship was closer to the Scilly Isles. In the Royal Navy, keeping such a log by so junior a seaman was treachery, but the sailor felt the danger was so great he had to alert the senior officers. Blinded by the Navy's rules and ignoring the possible accuracy of the sailor's calculations Admiral Shovell had him immediately hanged for mutiny.

Disastrously for Sir Clowdisley and his fleet, the sailor was correct, and the ship swiftly approached the rocks off the Scilly Isles. Sir Clowdisley's ship, the *Association,* struck first and in total four of the five ships were lost with 2,000 men drowned. One of the few survivors, Admiral Sir Clowdisley Shovell himself, was washed ashore and in his exhausted state was found by a local woman who promptly killed him for the emerald ring on his finger.

The Danger of Accepting Yesterday's Paradigms

Don't be afraid to question everything. What was true yesterday may not be true today. Researchers did an experiment with a pike and a tank full of minnows. Swimming around, the pike had all the minnows he could eat. After a few days they separated the pike from the minnows with a glass partition. He could see the minnows but could not reach them through this invisible barrier. After twelve hours he gave up. The researchers removed the glass. The pike had free access once again to the minnows. Even though they were now all around him and still believing them inaccessible, he made no attempt to eat them and eventually starved to death.

The Monkey and the Banana

A similar experiment starts with a cage containing five apes. Hanging from the top of the cage is a bunch of bananas. Underneath is a stepladder. Wait until one of the monkeys goes to climb the ladder to get the bananas. As he climbs, spray him and all the other apes with ice-cold water. Each time one climbs the ladder, spray them all. It won't take long for the rest of them to stop any ape from going near the ladder.

With me so far? Here's the interesting part. Replace any ape with a new one. He will spot the bananas and go to climb the ladder. The other four will gather round and, to his shock and horror, attack him. A few such attacks will teach him to avoid the ladder. Replace another of the original apes with a new one. The remaining three and the first new ape will attack him as he goes for the bananas. The first newcomer will eagerly join in the assault without even knowing why. Keep going until you have replaced all the original apes. None of them will ever get to the bananas even though not one of them has been sprayed with water. It will be as if the ladder weren't there. It is "company policy" never to use the ladder.

You will frequently find that circumstances change. So do not be afraid to come back at a problem. A salesman calling on a potential account might suddenly discover he is in the right place at the right time, purely by keeping regularly in touch. Perhaps a new purchaser has taken over who is more amenable to the product.

That is not to say you should doggedly stay on a project if you are making no progress. Doing the same thing and expecting a different result is not a sign of intelligence. Question the circumstances and question your own beliefs concerning the topic or project. You might well be surprised at what you discover.

Einstein's Questions

Einstein's assistant could not believe what he saw. The great genius was setting the same questions for the physics exam that he had set the previous year. How could he be so lazy as not to think up new questions? He voiced his concern about the repetition to Einstein, who replied, "Yes, but the answers have changed."

"Believe those who are seeking the truth. Doubt those who find it."
Andre Gide

Pardon

Here in Ireland in the last few years a large number of soldiers and ex-soldiers have been taking the Irish Ministry of Defence to court. These men claim that their hearing was damaged, in many instances very seriously. Their argument is that the detonation from the guns used in their training and practice was so loud and so consistent that this led to loss of hearing. The Army had refused to provide protective ear coverings and would not permit the soldiers to use their own – as it was not official Army issue.

A friend of mine who was in the Irish shooting team thirty-five years ago told me of a demonstration his club were invited to give in the Curragh Camp, an Army base about thirty miles from Dublin. As they were preparing he noticed that his hosts, the soldiers, were not wearing ear protectors, as he and his teammates were. He queried this. "We aren't provided with any and although we bought our own, we were ordered not to use them," was the response.

The current Minister has been creating a great fuss about the soldiers who are claiming damages for hearing loss. He is giving out about the size of the claims made by the judges; that greedy solicitors are encouraging claims; how much the whole affair will cost the Government and ultimately the taxpayer.

Not once have I heard him or any official question or condemn the rules of an army, which would show such lack of concern for the men in its care. No former Minister for Defence or General has been asked to account for such a stupid rule – a rule which must defy all logic and common sense – and which in my opinion amounts to negligence. And that brings us to the power and purpose of institutions.

"Naked emperors everywhere you look."

The Institutions of Destitution

> ***"The purpose of institutions is to control and maintain power in their domain."* (Ed Stracher)**

Ed Stracher developed a very powerful speed-reading system. Some of his students can read almost as fast as they can turn the pages; others can even read two books at once. Everyone who learned the system was delighted. Even the slower students showed improvements that were, at the very least, remarkable.

He showed his results to the schools and universities. They unanimously turned him down. It would upset the status quo. Pupils would get through the course in less than half the time. A three-year course could be completed in a year. Universities would be receiving only a fraction of the fees, as pupils would be in attendance for only a fraction of the time.

The Lazy Teacher

One of my teachers in school had his pupils in little boxes. The good workers, the messers and the lazy ones. The grades you got for your homework reflected his idea of you. The good students always got good grades – regardless of the quality of their work. The other pupils received grades which reflected the teacher's opinion of them.

To test this, one of the brighter boys submitted his homework, which was deliberately poorly crafted, full of misspelling, bad punctuation and grammar. When the homework was returned after being apparently checked by the master, he found he had his usual 'A.' The boy stood up and questioned him. He pointed out his 'A' and then one of the mistakes. The teacher glossed over it. He pointed out a few more mistakes until the teacher realised that he had been caught out. The teacher called in the headmaster, who gave the pupil a severe dressing down for embarrassing the teacher.

You might think the principal would say, "I'm sorry, boys, but such standards are not acceptable from the teaching staff." No – he chose to protect the institution and reprimand the pupil, more for poking fun at its own glossy exterior than for anything else. So be aware that institutions will always cover their butts first. Have you ever heard an institution say, "I'm sorry, we made a mistake"?

Who Has the Answers to Your Medical Problem? Something You Should Know in Case You are Ever Ill

Doctors, surgeons and specialist medical consultants are highly respected members of our society. In tribal cultures, the medicine man, witch doctor or herbalist was equally, if not more, revered. Being in the position of curing the sick and preventing death is a highly responsible position.

As a teenager I had two visits with consultants. The first for an infection in my leg caused by stepping on broken glass while swimming in a river. The second was having my appendix removed. About 100 or 150 years ago, I might not have survived my teenage years, so I, for one, do appreciate medical advances. The average life expectancy has risen from thirty to well into the seventies and is increasing all the time. We do owe a great debt to modern medicine.

Medical associations and drug companies have very little interest in folk remedies and homeopathic medicine. By controlling prescribed medicines the doctors are protecting their niche and their power. This is not to knock doctors, but to point out that there can be viable alternatives.

If you go to a doctor and he prescribes a medicine, he

makes money, the pharmacist makes money and the drug companies make money. This in itself is good. The drug company employs people and invests time and effort in research and development, the results of which may find cures for diseases and infections. The pharmacist and doctor have a spouse, family and business to keep and run, and hopefully you get better.

Professionals are looked upon as authority figures. Doctors, lawyers, architects, accountants. We look up to them and if we have a question for them we generally accept and respect their answer. Certainly you would hope they would want what is best for you. You are paying them for their valued opinion. You would expect the best advice available.

Doctors are there to care for you and hopefully cure you. Now we know that doctors can sometimes be wrong. Why? Doctors work very long hours. Apart from the long years they spent studying in medical school, there is so much new medical knowledge becoming available. New surgical techniques, advances in drugs, new equipment, all of which has to be mastered. Seventy per cent of the drugs or medicines in the marketplace were not around fifteen years ago. So how is the doctor to keep abreast of what is new and relevant?

According to Dr Gerry Avron, associate professor at Harvard Medical School: "The education of the American physician about drugs has been relegated to the drug companies by default. As a result, pharmacological solutions are thought of first rather than non-pharmacological approaches that could be just as effective and even safer."

In a test at the Harvard Medical School, doctors were given some medical journals and magazines to read and study. Questioning the doctors afterwards they found them more influenced by the advertising from the drug companies than by the editorial content. The doctors concerned could not believe these findings – that they were being influenced by non-scientific sources!

All drugs that come new to the marketplace may not be

fully tested. The drug companies have to comply with statutory laws, but they cannot cover long-term testing with the general public, and unfortunately some drugs have long-term consequences and side effects.

I know if I were a doctor it would be almost impossible to keep abreast of the medical developments. So it is important for you to be vigilant in questioning your doctor about his prescription, his experience with similar prescriptions and the possible alternatives.

There is another dimension to the medical drug problem. People expect to be prescribed drugs. I have discussed this with doctors. Patients expect and frequently demand a wonder drug to cure their ailment. They do not want to be told to lose weight, amend their diet, give up smoking and cut down on drinking.

Caveat Emptor

Just because someone is an authority figure and has lots of credentials and degrees, it is no reason to accept what they say without question. Certainly, in their area of expertise, they will have considerably more authority than the average man in the street. If you consult an expert, then his or her advice should not be dismissed lightly. You do need to analyse with your conscious mind all the information, and then let your intuitive side stew it over before giving you the answer. You have to decide what is right for you. As American business philosopher Jim Rohn says, "Whatever conclusion you come to, make sure it is your own."

Apologise? No Way!

Occasionally though, doctors do err. Patients may be misdiagnosed or have the wrong treatment prescribed. Or perhaps in the heat of the moment there may be an error of judgement. The results could mean permanent disability or even death. Now the interesting thing is that I have never heard of a doctor or hospital apologising for their error.

Watching a TV programme about medical mistakes, the patients, or the relatives of patients, who took successful legal action against hospitals all said the same thing. "We just wanted them to acknowledge us and give an apology. We are not doing it for the money."

In 1998 I read an article about the family of a young man who joined the parachute regiment of the British Army. His last jump was fatal. The family assumed it was an accident. A few weeks later, talking with one of their son's friends, it transpired that their son was unwell for two days before the jump. He had been completely disorientated, which was obvious to everyone. He had fallen asleep in class and later in his bunk slept for sixteen hours. He was in no condition for any work, never mind parachuting. Hearing this the family contacted the barracks and the Ministry of Defence. They got nowhere and their path was blocked at every turn. They resorted to legal action, which took six years. All they wanted, his family said, was an apology. They did get compensation, but no apology.

Beware the Man With the Key

There is one type who is not open to discussion, logic or reasoning. At the banquet, the honoured guest speaker asked his waiter for an extra pat of butter. "Sorry sir, it's only one pat per diner." "Do you know who I am?" inquired the speaker. "I have been invited along to speak after the meal by the managing director. It is because of me they are having this dinner." "And do you know who I am?" responded the waiter. "I am the man in charge of the butter."

Yes, it's what I call "the man with the key". The person who will not permit a reasonable request. It's the man in the uniform – the gatekeeper, who will not let you pass.

The best way to deal with these is to bow and scrape a little. Now really, do you want to be right or do you want to be effective? Another way, is to pull rank, contact their superior and explain the situation.

Turning up at an engagement in a hall some years ago my stage manager and I met the caretaker. We were impressed with the lighting for the hall. However, he told us he was in charge of it, and as it hadn't been arranged in advance, we couldn't use it. I was about to go into the bowing and scraping bit when my stage manager threw his hands in the air, walked around shouting at no one in particular, "Oh my God, it's the man with the key – it's the man with the key!" Whether "the man with the key" thought he was dealing with a lunatic or not, I don't know, but we got to use the lights!

Early in his professional career, top German magical entertainer Ted Lesley was booked to perform at a private function in the home of a major businessman. The butler opened the enormous front door. Ted announced himself, to be told to use the servant's entrance around the back. Now Ted was getting a very good fee and he did need the money but he did perceive himself as someone equal with his clients, not a servant.

He handed the butler his business card and said, "Tell Herr X that I called to fulfil my engagement. I am going back to my hotel. If Herr X wants me he can send a chauffeur." Ted left and thirty minutes later the chauffeur collected him from his hotel. At times you have to let people know how you expect to be treated.

The Owners of Truth

In your life, your endeavours, your play and your recreation, you will regularly meet people who tell you that you have to do this, or you can't do that. Frequently they will quote passages from the Bible, or quote a famous person as if to say, "That's all the proof you need." People are always quoting the Bible as though it were gospel. For your own interest and education I highly recommend you read the Bible from cover to cover. You will find passages that are regularly quoted out of context, sections that contradict other sections but you will also find deep wisdom and guidance. It is more than a fascinating historical document, it is more than knowledge, it is about life.

Do not spend time arguing with these people. You are giving them control over you. The philosopher E.M. Cioran covers these points in his book *A Short History of Decay.* " [Man's] power to adore is responsible for all his crimes: a man who loves a god unduly forces other men to love his god, eager to exterminate them if they refuse … once man loses his *faculty of indifference* he becomes a potential murderer ... We kill only in the name of a god or his counterfeits. … In every mystic outburst, the moans of victims parallel the moans of ecstasy … scaffolds, dungeons, jails flourish only in the shadow of a faith – of that need to believe which has infested the mind forever. The devil pales beside the man who owns a truth, his truth …"

You are not likely to hear the following passage from the Bible read out in church. This is what Jesus himself had to say about the owners of truth, referring to the Pharisees: *"Do not, however, imitate their actions because they don't practice what they preach. They tie onto people's backs loads that are heavy and hard to carry, yet they aren't willing to lift a finger to help them carry those loads. They do everything so that people will see them. They love the best places at feasts and the reserved seats in the synagogues. They love to be greeted with respect in the market places and to be called teacher. How terrible for you, teachers of the law and Pharisees: you hypocrites: you sail the seas and cross whole countries to win one convert: and when you succeed, you make him twice as deserving of going to hell as you yourselves are! How terrible for you, teachers of the law and Pharisees! You hypocrites! You clean the outside of your cup and plate, while the inside is full of what you have obtained by violence and selfishness. Blind Pharisee! Clean what is inside the cup first and then the outside will be clean too!*

"How terrible for you, teachers of the law and Pharisees! You hypocrites! You are like whitewashed tombs, which look fine on the outside but are full of bones and decaying corpses on the inside. In the same way on the outside you appear good to everybody, but inside you are full of hypocrisy and sins."

The Floor Sweeper

A young man, hired by a supermarket, reported for his first day of work. The manager greeted him with a warm handshake and a smile, gave him a broom and said, "Your first job will be to sweep out the store."

"But I'm a college graduate!" the young man replied indignantly.

"Oh, I'm sorry, I didn't know that," said the manager. "Here, give me the broom, I'll show you how."

"The most useless (and usually poor) people on earth are those so smart who can spell h-o-r-s-e in seven languages but so dumb, they'd buy a cow to ride." **Dan Kennedy**

"You can be the best garbage man or the best model – it doesn't matter as long as you're the best."
Muhammed Ali

CHAPTER 12

Your Subconscious Mind in Business

No one on his deathbed says, "I wish I'd spent more time at the office."

The age when you went to work for a company aged eighteen, and stayed until sixty-five is over.

During your career you may work at many different jobs or you might work at the same job and regularly change employers. Realise that, whatever you do, you are working not for your company or your boss, but for you. You are working for you. Yes, you are self-employed. You are the managing director of "Me Limited". You may well get a weekly or monthly paycheque from the place you work but in reality you are a free agent. Like professional footballers, you are selling yourself to the highest bidder. If you don't like it where you are you can go elsewhere.

The main difference between a job and being self-employed is that in regular employment you have just one contract, while a person normally perceived as being self-employed has as many contracts as clients.

If you are self-employed or high up in the business world you will learn strategies and techniques in this chapter that would be of great benefit to your bottom line, the success of your business and the quality of your work environment. If you are in a regular job you will learn to go beyond the mindset that "employees only do enough work to avoid being fired and employers only pay enough to stop the workers going elsewhere." If you are seeking work you will find ideas that, if implemented, will make you a desirable commodity in the marketplace.

Many people work in a business that does not suit who they really are. It is like wearing someone else's shoes. Did you know the biggest cause of stress in people under the age of sixty-five is working in a job they hate?

Vocation or Avocation

Some people look to their job for income and their hobby for fulfilment. Many of the great discoveries came from an avocation during playtime or hobby time. Here is a quote from Henry Ford's now defunct Dearborn Independent: "The father of photography was an army officer; and of the electric motor a bookbinder's clerk. The inventor of the telegraph was a portrait painter; the jacquard loom, a dressmaker. A farmer invented the typewriter; a poet, the sewing machine; a cabinetmaker the cotton gin; and a coalminer the locomotive. The telephone was the after-school work of a teacher of the deaf; the disc talking machine, the night work of a clothing salesman; the wax cylinder phonograph, of a lawyer's clerk; the typesetting machine a grocery man. A doctor made the first pneumatic tyre because his little son was an invalid. The story of many great inventions has been the result of somebody riding a hobby."

A Recipe for Success

You are looking for ways to build your income or get wealthy. Mix a tablespoon of creativity, a cup of thinking, two heaps of observation and a sprinkling of intuition. That is the basic recipe. Here are more details.

Business schools teach you to look for needs in the marketplace. They are partly correct. You must look for wants in the marketplace. You might need a new pair of shoes, but want a pair of designer trainers. You might need a new sink, but want the latest CD. When television sets came on the market in the United States in the 1950s, they outsold refrigerators by more than two to one, especially to people in lower income areas who had no refrigerators. They wanted the televisions more than they needed the refrigerators.

Basic rule: look for a want in the marketplace. When you find the want, don't wait too long to fill it. It is a slap in the face to come up with an idea, agree with yourself it is good, and not to run with it; then a year or two later you find that someone else got the same idea, put it into the marketplace and now hardly has time to count the shekels.

Start with the area you love most. Make a list of every product or service to do with it. Ask yourself what could be done to improve the service, the product or the packaging of it. It is always easier, cheaper and infinitely more profitable to improve an existing product than to invent, produce and market a brand new one.

Coming to the marketplace with something brand new can be really expensive because you have to sell the idea for the product first, before you sell the product itself. When fax machines came out, it took quite a while for them to take off. People had to get used to the idea first. It was new technology, a new piece of machinery. More recently, the plain paper fax machines were introduced. Hey, what a great idea! No rolls of special paper. The marketplace can grasp the improved concept instantly. In fact, fax machine users may well have been saying for years, "Wouldn't it be great if they came up with a fax machine using ordinary paper?"

In your work or hobby, have you developed an idea or system that could be marketed through that industry? To ask the question is to set your subconscious to work.

How to Succeed in a Saturated Marketplace

Can you do well in a saturated marketplace? Let us say you are going to open a coffee shop, but your area is already overcrowded. There is strong competition. How would you proceed?

Ask the question, "How do I make money here?"

Instead of opening a shop yourself why not supply the coffee shops? Sell them something. A special brand of aromatic coffee. A cost-saving coffee-making machine. Self-cleaning cups. Self-cleaning machines. Find something already existing or develop something new. You can always make a fortune from people who are making a fortune. While the gold miners are knee deep in mud panning for gold, you can be the one on dry land selling them their pans, shovels and clothing. Real fortunes were made this way in the Old West. Levi Jeans are just one example. Make your fortune selling to those who are making theirs.

Sell Your Knowledge

Have you developed a system or procedure for doing something efficiently in your business? You can sell or franchise the system to others outside your market area. That is what a franchise is – you are selling a working system. If they buy it, they work your system and get your results. The franchisees are buying a system that works. All the snags have already been removed. A franchised business is ten times less likely to go under than a brand new business starting off.

This is what happens with McDonald's – it was the genius of Ray Kroc, a salesman who saw what the McDonald Brothers had – a system. When you take a McDonald's franchise you learn the philosophy and work the system. Providing you don't deviate from the system, you will get the same results as all the other McDonald's restaurants.

Golden rule of change in business: every time there is a major shift in technology, social interest or the law, somebody gets rich.

Take computers. Each time there is a breakthrough who makes the money? Well, the manufacturers, the suppliers, the trainers, the manual writers including the companies who produce books like *Computers for Dummies*, the support people. And of course the research people are back working on the next new wave of technology. When the tax laws change, accountants make more money. When the government brings out a new law, somebody writes a book and makes money from it.

So whatever your industry is, there is constant growth and change. Train yourself to be alert for opportunity. You don't have to analyse every detail of every situation. Just tell yourself that you are looking for opportunity. Keep your eyes open, be curious and the opportunity will find you.

Ne Illegitimati Carborundum Est

Bureaucracy comes from the French and means "Rule of the desk or office". Rules, regulations, regular routine and office politics build up around your desk. People take breaks and take time for a gossip. People are under the misguided impression that they work at their desks. Desks have a number of functions, hardly any of which are productive:

1. They attract clutter. Papers mount up into bundles, to be dealt with – tomorrow, which turns out to be next week, next month, next year. The bundles turn into little mountains, and the bigger they grow the more daunting is the task to sort through them, and clutter is a major obstacle to flow in your life.
2. Desks give the illusion of accomplishment under the cover of meaningless activity. You can spend all day at your desk, be busy, busy, busy and achieve virtually nothing, moving papers around, reading the newspaper, taking a tea break, discussing the next meeting.
3. Desks hinder creative thinking while at best focusing on conscious, logical thinking. Desk thinking inhibits the developing of fresh ideas, while dampening any sign of progress. It will not give the subconscious the chance to function. Deskbound thinking is responsible for more poor plans, bad decisions and faulty business judgement than anything else. Worse still, it favours discussing the problem rather than solving it. Frequently, no decision gets made at all.

Ninety-nine per cent of the right solutions will NOT come while you are at your desk. Remember, you are paid for accomplishment, not to be at your desk. If you must have a desk, have it in an awkward uncomfortable place so that you will be more inclined to stay away from it than be at it.

Business Decision Making

Rule 1 has just been covered: Avoid desks. Remember, this alone will improve your accomplishment and efficiency by at least one hundred per cent and improve your decision making so much; you will be like a new man or woman.

Rule 2: Do not strive to be too rational and logical. This kind of thinking, which is taught in business schools and encouraged in hierarchical businesses, is flawed. It must be used with the subconscious and the superconscious.

Rule 3: Put your time to good use. The common perception of work is nine to five, and then forget about it until the next day. What is not generally realised is the hours you don't work are as important as the hours you do work.

How To Work the Hours You Don't Work

"What?" I hear you ask. "Surely, Quentin, you don't want me to be working while I am at home as well?" Generations ago, twelve- to fourteen-hour days of hard physical labour were not just the norm, but necessary. As time went by, machines were invented to handle the backbreaking toil. This trend is continuing. Word processors took over from typewriters, making corrections and duplicate pages so easy. Now it looks as though voice-activated software will in turn replace the physical skills of typing.

The underlying trend here is that people who are using their minds are the ones who are getting rich. You do not have to be an inventor or developer. You just need to let your mind work on the problem. If you are in the fortunate position of not having any immediate problems, then look for opportunities to improve the systems you already have. Ask yourself how you can make things better. How could you make the systems more efficient? What would we have to do to get ten per cent better results from ...?

So getting back to the hours you don't work. If you have an eight-hour working day, you should work for no more than six, including your lunch break. Go and play golf, read a book, doze off, walk along the beach, wash the dishes. Give yourself a break. Getting into the quiet countryside or sitting beside the sea is a wonderful way of calming the mind and stimulating the creative process. The Finnish composer Jean Sibelius preferred hustle. Here's what he had to say:

"I wished to hear what new things were being performed out there in the wider world, and in any case I had a lot of plans that I wanted to think about in peace and quiet. My previous trips abroad had taught me that spending time in large cities did wonders for my creative powers. Living in a great metropolis has always meant the same to me as living in the middle of the Sahara. Disappear into the crowd and you can concentrate entirely on yourself."

By using only your conscious mind at your place of business, you work it too hard and it overloads, resulting in flawed decisions. You need to bring your intuitive side into the process and it is as simple as this. You start the process with your conscious mind, define your objective, study and think about all the available data and then let it go. Stop thinking about it. Let your subconscious go to work on the backburner. The solution will come. Don't rush it. It may take a few minutes, hours, days or weeks, but it will come – out of the blue. The solution will be so clean-cut and will come with such utter conviction that you can act instantly with the assurance you are right.

You will accomplish more in six hours of work if you will only learn how to use the other eighteen. The six hours are for work, defining the problems, assembling the data, accomplishing what you can. The other eighteen are for letting go and allowing your subconscious to work.

The Four-Week Coffee Break

Beware of the coffee break syndrome. A ten or fifteen-minute coffee break usually drags on for twenty to thirty minutes. Two twenty-minute breaks a day is forty minutes. Over five working days that is 200 minutes which when added up equal four working weeks a year. Could you put this time to better use? Better than killing time, gossiping or discussing last night's soaps? How about a short break to give your subconscious a chance to stew things over?

> ***"If I had eight hours to cut down a tree, I would spend the first six sharpening the saw."* (Abraham Lincoln)**

But the eighteen hours of not working will go to waste if you do not programme your mind during the six hours, by asking yourself the right questions before handing over to the subconscious. The wife of William Faulkner, the author, could not accept that he was working when he was sitting still looking out of the window. She didn't realise that it was from this contemplation that his best ideas came.

Sometimes talking things over with a friend or spouse will help settle your mind. During the American Civil War, Abraham Lincoln sent for one of his top generals. He wanted to ask his advice. The general later reported that Lincoln asked him to sit down and for the next two hours, proceeded to talk through his plans for the war. At the end, he thanked the general for his help. Yet the general had contributed nothing. Lincoln just talked through the whole time until he was happy in his own mind he had the right answer.

Here is a tip for handling correspondence. If you have a lot of letters and are dictating replies as you go along, you will come to one and not be sure how to respond. Just place it to the bottom of the pile and continue. When you come back to it your subconscious, having mulled it over, will give you the right reply.

Be grateful for challenges. If it were not for the things that go wrong with your job you wouldn't have one. Everything would run so smoothly that someone further down the ladder could replace you on a much lower paycheque.

Four Steps to Swift Effective Decisions

> ***"Wealthy people make decisions quickly and change their minds slowly, if at all."* (Napoleon Hill)**

Making a decision removes uncertainty from your life. It frees your mind. You flip onto a new frequency of thought when you decide. This new frequency will in turn tune into and attract people, locations and events to advance you. It sounds completely illogical, but when you go with the flow, you get there quicker.

Here are four questions to ask yourself next time you have a decision to make. If the answer is yes, proceed to the following question.

1. Do I want to be, do or have this?
2. Will being, doing or having this move me in the direction of my goal?
3. Is being, doing or having this in harmony with God's laws or the laws of the universe?
4. Will being, doing or having this violate the rights of others?

One of the biggest problems in companies today is actually getting employees to solve a problem as it arises, without having to go to a manager or somebody higher up. Managers are busy managing, and bosses are busy running companies. So they shouldn't be dealing with every small problem that arises. Not solving problems as they crop up results in a lot of wasted time and money. It creates clutter, blockage and stagnation.

Forward-thinking companies have given their employees the power to solve whatever problems they come across. If as a customer of the Ritz Carlton Hotel you approach an employee with a problem, he or she, be they room cleaner or bellboy, is empowered to spend up to $2,000 to solve it.

Unfortunately, too many bosses and managers do not trust their staff or their workers. Of course it is vital that new employees be shown how things do work in a company, but they should also be trusted to make the right decision when problems arise. If the attitude of management is that the employees are too stupid to make the right decision, the employees will never make any decision, whether right or wrong. Should they do, it will be likely to be the wrong one, because that is what is expected of them; the management believes them to be stupid so they are fulfilling the expectation.

The Steps to Better Business Decisions (When You Have More Time)

1. Stop relying on rational thought alone.

2. Realise you need to use both your rational and intuitive sides.

3. Define the problem.

4. Assemble data.

5. Logically attack the problem.

6. Let it go. The key to the subconscious is relaxation.

7. Get out of the office. Play golf. Take a walk. Indulge in your hobby.

Conscious logical decisions tend to be wrong because they leave out some vital factor. On the other hand, intuitive decisions are related to the whole underlying process of life and the universe.

What To Do When You Simply Can't Decide What To Do Next

Ever find you can't make up your mind what to do next? Perhaps there is a list of tasks and you aren't sure how to prioritise them? Maybe you have finished a major project and are undecided what to start or where to turn. The solution is easy but not simple. Only the top five per cent will embrace it.

Do what you fear the most.

That's it.

How a Top Recording Company Chose Their No. 1 Hits

Have you ever heard of the Old Grey Whistle Test? A major record company narrowed down a handful of songs to be released. They felt these songs had hit potential. But which one to go with? They invited in the cleaner who was known as "Old Grey". He would listen to the songs and whichever tune he whistled as he left was the one the company went with and it invariably reached the top. If Old Grey whistled it, that was it!

Building a Church: How Long Should It Take?

Herbert Quick told the story of Deidrich Knickerbocker's great-grandfather, who won the contract to build a church in Rotterdam. He spent three months smoking, considering the task. Another three months visiting every church on the journey from Rotterdam, through Amsterdam, Delft, Haarlem, Leyden, The Hague and back to Rotterdam. He spent another three months walking around and studying the site from every angle.

The citizens of Rotterdam were getting the jitters at the apparent lack of progress. Still, it was another three months of contemplation before he pulled off his coat and laid the cornerstone of the church.

According to the great historian of New Amsterdam when the church was completed, "All the zealous Christians of Rotterdam preferred it to any other."

Would You Have Seen the Opportunity?

Having been with the company, Cartan, O'Meara and Kieran for three years, solicitor John Schütte read about new technology hitting the marketplace. He hadn't seen one but, from what he read, he could see the potential. It was word processors. He could see it would save a lot of repetitive typing. In the long run, it would be cheaper; it could mass-produce and give better quality documents. Definitely, he felt, this was the way forward. John and his boss's secretaries could share the machine. However, his boss rejected the idea.

Not being easily put off, John returned to his boss with a different proposal. John would buy the word processor himself. Now, back then the price of a word processor was pretty close to John's annual salary. His boss would deduct the lease repayments from John's monthly paycheque. His boss could also use the machine. John felt by using the processor he would be freeing time that could be used for bringing in other work, which would lead to a higher salary, thus paying for the machine. In other words, John would bear all the risk of the cost of the machine, it would cost the firm nothing, and they would get the use of it. His boss's response was, "That's not the way we do things here."

With this attitude, John felt that there would be no future with that firm and decided to go out on his own. After a few years of general practice he decided to concentrate on one area of law. He built the largest specialist personal injury firm in the Republic of Ireland and was the first solicitor in Europe to bring in the "no win no fee" concept for his clients, thus, carrying over his intuitive concept of risk reversal.

An offshoot of this story is that three months after he decided to specialise, a client came in with a million-pound conveyance. It may not sound much now, but back then it was a large job with a very good fee. John thought for only a moment and referred the client elsewhere. He didn't want to be distracted back into what he had given up.

If he had accepted it, and it must have been tempting, he would have given clashing signals to his subconscious.

Integrity

Once you have made up your mind and proceed along your chosen path, integrity is vital to keep you on track. Don't be like the parent or boss who knows they need to lay down clear boundaries for behaviour, but they fear that an unpopular decision will hinder their own personal need for approval. Don't take on a client just because you need the money and you are not sure that you can help them.

In every field of endeavour, there is a block of work that is disliked, but necessary. Entrepreneurs detest paperwork but love the opportunities of business. Accountants revel in paperwork and dislike risk-taking. Government departments love designing forms and having meetings and initiating enquiries, but when it comes to making decisions ... well, you get the point.

If your attitude is I am only going to do my job within the parameters laid down and that is all you are doing, then you are condemned to extinction. Change in business, attitudes and technology will make you obsolete. Where you are right now, you may hate your work or hate an aspect of it. But instead, consider it an opportunity for advancement. If you don't like what you are doing, use it as a chance for growth. If you are digging ditches and don't love your work, use your logical and intuitive minds to figure out ways of doing it so well that you will automatically go up.

The Dishwasher

Top motivational speaker Anthony Robbins tells of going on a two-week retreat in a remote area of India. Each participant was given a menial task to be done for four hours each day. He was assigned to washing dishes. Since a child he hated washing dishes – he detested the task with a vengeance. After one and a half hours of moaning and complaining he realised that unless he changed his attitude, it would be sheer hell for the next two weeks. So he developed the mindset of being the best dishwasher they ever had. His enthusiasm spread to the other dishwashers. Putting their minds to it, they got through more dishes quicker and faster than anyone else, while having great fun doing so.

Developing the Right Mindset

If you approach any activity with a mindset of doing it well, it will open endless opportunities in your business and personal life. It will stimulate your creative muscles, your thinking muscles and your intuitive side.

In spite of what most people think, it is not difficult to be above average and it requires only marginal thought and minimal creativity. Yes, it requires more to go well beyond that, but take it one step at a time. In most cases, it needs only care and attention to basic details to rise above the mediocre who are always at their best.

Showing Up

Woody Allen said that eighty per cent of success is showing up. Showing up on time is even better. A few months ago I decided to have some professional photographs taken of me. Feeling it would be worthwhile considering a new hairstyle for the photos, I phoned an agent who recommended a stylist who does the hair of many contemporary Irish pop stars, models and celebrities. I called to make an appointment with him. He said he was quite busy but next week would be better, and could I phone on Monday when he would know his schedule.

Monday morning I called back. Yes, I could have a slot on Thursday at 10.30am or 2.30pm. I chose 10.30.

Arriving at 10.25, I was told he had just slipped out and would be back in a few minutes. I waited until 10.45. No sign of him. I left. And I was not a happy camper. Now, had he been with another client and was running late, I would have understood. Likewise, he could have been stuck in traffic. But no, knowing I was coming in at a time that suited him, he, already on the premises, left. He did not show up. Not only did his firm, one of the largest in Ireland, lose the business of my first – and now only visit, but also lost the regular monthly visits that would have occurred had I been happy with the initial outcome.

Once running a theatre show, I wanted some photos of the occasion. They could be taken over a ten-day period. The photographer was to come on a Friday. At the last minute, he couldn't make it. His schedule was busy, so we settled on the following Thursday or, failing that, the following Monday which would be the last opportunity. He assured me he would be there on the Thursday. He did not turn up. That was okay as the Monday was still on. I left a message on his answering machine reminding him of the Monday.

Sunday night I phoned and got him. He wouldn't be able to make it. A big job had come in. During the ensuing conversation, it turned out he had known about this since the previous week, and had not told me. "Don't give me a hard time," he said, "this is my big chance." I said I was delighted for him, but if he had told me, even the previous Friday, I could have arranged for another photographer. He hung up.

Interestingly, through our office, he had booked an entertainer for his child's party a few months earlier. His wife phoned up three times to make sure the entertainer would turn up on time. We thought this a bit strange. Now we know why. She is well used to her husband's commitment keeping! Remember the plumbers from Chapter 4 with the ad "We Show Up"? No wonder they would do so well! Fortunately I have since found an excellent photographer who did the cover photos for this book.

Four-Mula for Success

Canadian business consultant Dan Sullivan has four rules for business success:

1. Show up on time.
2. Do what you say you will do.
3. Finish what you start.
4. Say please and thank you.

Just doing number one will put you ahead of the game. Doing all four simple steps will put you way ahead of your competition. If you can rise above the norm purely by showing up and, when you do, set about your work to make it both fun and productive, imagine what you can achieve by adding some thought, creativity and intuition?

Could You Turn Your Business Around, and Work Half the Time At Twice the Money?

Are you aware that dentists have a high suicide rate? People associate dentists with pain, injections, clinical procedures and drills in their mouths. If you have ever had a dentist's probe hit a raw nerve, you know what I mean. So while people may personally like their dentist, they hate going and hate being there. These feelings communicate themselves to the dentist, consciously or unconsciously, and bit by bit affect his self-esteem. Well, would you like working with clients who hated being there and couldn't wait to get away?

Paddi Lund, a dentist from Brisbane, Australia, was deeply unhappy with his work. Twenty per cent of his patients were unpunctual and didn't pay attention to their teeth. His unhappiness gave way to severe depression, bordering on the suicidal. He asked himself the question, "If the goal of life is happiness, why am I spending the prime hours of the prime years of my life in a job that does not give me happiness?"

To ask the question is to set the subconscious and intuitive areas to work. He considered his choices. He could change career but he really wanted to be a dentist. How could he stay a dentist and yet be happy, really happy? He would have to change the way he did business. The Pareto principle certainly applied. Twenty per cent of his clients gave him eighty per cent of his problems. So he decided to get rid of them by referring them to other dentists. He would keep his best patients, and gradually weed out any others who were not up to scratch by replacing them with better clients who would be accepted into the practice by referral only. He took his name out of the Yellow Pages and the telephone book, closed the door and put a notice outside "BY REFERRAL ONLY". He did no advertising at all. All clients had to agree to turn up on time, pay on the day of the visit, get a regular check-up and take care of their teeth.

When you arrive at Paddi's practice, you are greeted by your first name, and shown into one of three rooms, each of which has an armchair, a coffee table and your favourite newspaper. They have taken the trouble, in advance, to find out from the person who referred you what is your favourite newspaper, your favourite coffee and what your first name is. Not just your first name but whether you would like to be addressed as Quentin or Mr

Reynolds. A card on the door of the inner room says, "Reserved for Quentin Reynolds".

There is no reception desk, no official waiting room, and no pungent patient alarming smells of formorresol and eugenol. Instead there is the aroma of fresh flowers, freshly baked muffins from their own kitchen and newly made percolating coffee. When the assistant returns to your room with tea or coffee and muffins, which is silver service, she knocks before entering. Remember it is not a waiting room, it is your room.

When you get to see Paddi he gives you a little buzzer to hold. If there is even the slightest pain, you press it and he will stop and won't proceed again until you are comfortable. When your visit is over you get a bag of your favourite muffins to take home with you.

Now, most people would not be able to tell the difference between the technical competencies of any two dentists. Paddi's philosophy is that if you are treated so well when you arrive in the small details that you can perceive, then they must be just as good with your teeth. When you pay attention to detail in non-business-related things, customers feel that you must be providing quality goods or services.

Paddi now works less than twenty-five hours a week and earns double the average Australian dentist's salary.

Paddi wrote a book about the whole experience called *Building the Happiness Centred Business*. It is available by referral only. Details are at the back of the book. Tell them Quentin sent you.

Look After Your Best Friend

Your business is your best friend. It pays for your house, your medical expenses, your food and your vacations. Look on it as a family member but don't neglect your family in pursuit of the business. Here are four true stories. The first three are from the May 1999 issue of *Worth Magazine*. The last I relate from first-hand experience.

Orlando, Florida: It is three in the morning. Michael Eisner, CEO of Disney, and his assistant climb over a fence onto property belonging to his competitor Universal Studios. He wants to check for signs of construction on the apparently vacant site.

A photograph from his trip to Egypt shows M. Douglas Ivester, CEO of Coca-Cola, among a group of tourists. All the tourists are taking in the breathtaking sights of the Valley of the Kings. Ivester is staring into a rubbish bin counting the empty Coke cans.

Millard Drexler, CEO, The Gap, hasn't worn a suit for over twenty-five years. He spends time in the stores checking the quality of the cloth and the colour of the buttons. He watches out for small details like whether the carpet on the floor looks too worn. He also asks groups of teenagers, on the street or in shopping centres, their opinions about clothing.

The Seeds You Sow

Over twenty years ago I was booked to do a show for the four-year-old son of supermarket boss Feargal Quinn. He had built his chain of stores up around quality service. More innovations took place in his Superquinn stores than any other supermarket. He was (and still is) regularly found on the floor of the shops talking to customers. Besides his business commitments, he is also now a Senator in the Dail, the Irish parliament. Anyway, the birthday party was on a Tuesday afternoon. I was very surprised to find him at home, playing with the children. Back then it was very unusual to find a father at a child's party on a weekday. Even at weekends fathers tended to head for the golf course at the crack of dawn, leaving the mother to manage as best she could.

The following year Mrs Quinn phoned to invite me back. This time, the party was to be on a Friday. I was already booked for the whole weekend. I suggested the

Thursday. In the background I could hear her and Feargal discussing this. He checked his diary, found he had a business meeting but said he would change it so he could attend the party and suit me. That is certainly balancing your business and family life.

As I said, the first party in his home was a Tuesday. The following Saturday I was performing at the home of another top Irish businessman. His son was ten years old. Now ten-year-olds can be fairly wild at a party. These kids were some of the nicest and most well-behaved I had ever come across. The birthday boy's father was not at home. It crossed my mind that only a few days previously a father had taken an afternoon off to be at his four-year-old's party, at an age when the youngster wouldn't really appreciate it. Here was a ten year old who would appreciate it and his father was absent. After I finished the show and was packing away, his dad arrived from the races in his chauffeur-driven limousine, his licence having been revoked for drunken driving. Fourteen years later, that same ten-year-old boy, now aged twenty-four was arrested for speeding under the influence of alcohol.

Plant the seed and the universe will give you the tree. Be careful what seeds you sow!

ACKNOWLEDGEMENTS

Special thanks to John Schutte for his help, advice and encouragement in writing this book.

Roisin O'Broin, my patient typist, Martin Breese of Breese Books in London for his technical help, John Bell for proofreading, Kate Davis for editing, Terry Willers, brilliant cartoonist, for his drawings, Adrienne Foran, Kathi Dunn for her patience, Burt Dubin, Richard Webster, Don Harper of Artwerk, Mark Reddy of Norton Associates for the cover photos, Eric and Muriel Sharp for steering me towards a career of fun and fulfillment, John Bowden and Tanya Kelly.

Chapter 1 *Acres of Diamonds* by Russell Conwell,

Chapter 2 *Paradigms* by Joel Barker.
The Peace Center, Theosophical Society in the Phillipines, 1 Iba Street, Quezon City, Phillipines.
Dr Willis Harman of the Institute of Noetic Sciences.

Chapter 4. *The Strategy of Pre-eminence* by Jay Abraham.

Chapter 6. *Secrets of Wealth* by Dan Lee Dimke.
How to Talk to Anyone, Anytime, Anywhere by Larry King.
WOW by Rob Gilbert Reprinted by permission. © 1999, Bits & Pieces, The Economics Press, Inc., 12 Daniel Road, Fairfield New Jersey 07004-2565 USA;
Phone: (+1 973)227-1224. FAX: (+1 973)227-9742.
E-mail: intl@epinc.com Web site: http://www.epinc.com

Chapter 7. Alexander Everett, Denis Stevenson.

Chapter 9. Peter Martin in The Sunday Times Magazine.

Chapter 11. Leo Enright in The Irish Times.
Longitude: The true story of a lone genius who solved the greatest scientific problem of his time by Dava Sobel

RECOMMENDED RESOURCES

Books:

Practical Intuition by Laura Day, published by Broadway Books. For your further intuitive development.

The Intuitive Manager by Roy Rowan. Little, Brown and Co.

Any of the books written by Stuart Wilde

The Five Day Course in Thinking by Edward de Bono. Superb for developing lateral thinking.

How to Make Millions with your Ideas by Dan Kennedy. The resource you need when your mind starts giving you those brilliant ideas. Penguin.

Chicken Soup for the Soul by Jack Canfield and Mark Victor Hansen. All of the Chicken Soup series of books are worth reading. Very inspiring.

Feng Shui. Richard Webster has a number of books on this subject published by Llewellyn

99% INSPIRATION by Bryan W. Mattimore, published by Amacom. This is an excellent book on creativity.

Pat Ingoldsby's Books of Poetry, published by Willow Publications, 3 Vernon Court, Dublin 3. Ireland. Funny, moving, sad and inspiring. A joy to read.

How to Develop a Super-Power Memory by Harry Lorayne. This is the best book on memory training ever written.

The Happiness Centred Business by Dr Paddi Lund, available only from: Solutions Press, 149 Old Cleveland Road, Capalaba, Queensland 4157 Australia. Tel: + 61 7 3823 3230 www.solutionspress.com.au

Magazines:

Intuition Magazine, 275 Brannan Street, 3rd Floor, San Francisco, CA 94107, USA Email: intuitmag@aol.com

Audio Tapes:

Nightingale Conant, 7300 North Lehigh Avenue, Niles, Illinois 60714, USA. Tel: 1-800-323-5552 or www.nightingale.com

Nightingale Conant, Long Road, Paignton, Devon TQ4 7BB, England. Tel: 01803 557148

Jim Rohn International: www.jimrohn.com He also publishes a free weekly e-zine.

Recommended audio recordings:
If you can only buy one then get The Psychology of Achievement.

The Psychology of Achievement by Brian Tracy
Lead the Field by Earl Nightingale
See You At the Top by Zig Ziglar
The Weekend Seminar by Jim Rohn
Journey to the Boundless by Deepak Chopra
The Awakened Life by Wayne Dyer
Lessons in Mastery by Anthony Robbins
Into the Genius Zone by Ed Stracher

Useful Websites:

Intuition:	www.mishlove.com www.quentinreynolds.com
Marketing:	www.abraham.com www.dankennedy.com
Audio recordings:	www.nightingale.com

Index

TO CONTACT THE AUTHOR

You can have Quentin Reynolds appear at your event.

He is available to present his workshop/seminar
"Your Intuitive Edge"

or his lively audience interactive show "Theatre of the Mind" which is perfect for meetings, promotions or after dinner entertainment.

Please phone: Int + 353 1 878 6331
or
Fax: Int + 353 1 872 0992

You can check out his website at
www.quentinreynolds.com

You may also write to him c/o the Publisher
Adventures In Astonishment,
134 Custom Hall
Deverell Place
Dublin 1
Ireland.

FREE REPORT
and ORDER FORM

To get a free report **Your Intuitive Edge** please fill out the form below and send it to:

Adventures In Astonishment
134 Custom Hall
Deverell Place
Dublin 1, Ireland

Please send me the following:

Your Intuitive Edge (free report) ❑

Intuition: Your Secret Power @ £15 ❑

Intuition: Your Action Plan (audio tape) ❑
by Quentin Reynolds @£10

Please add £2 shipping for the first book or tape and £1 for each additional book or tape sent anywhere in the world. The Free Report if ordered on its own is sent free anywhere in the world.

Your name: ______________________________

Company name: ______________________________

Address: ______________________________

City: ______________ State: ___________

Postcode (Zip): ______________________________

Telephone ______________________________
(in case we have a question about your order):